The Essential Handbook For Personal Assistants

Tools For Becoming Or Hiring The Ultimate Personal Assistant

By C.S. Copeland

Visit our Web site at www.PersonalAssistantGuide.com

Printed in the United States of America

First Printing: March 2009

Library of Congress Cataloging-in-Publication Data

Copeland, C.S.

    The Essential Handbook for Personal Assistants

    ISBN 978-1441496164

Contents

Part 3: - 72
Becoming A Kickass Personal Assistant

Chapter 5:
Killer Techniques For Making Yourself Invaluable! - 73

Chapter 6:
Preparing And Looking Like A Pro - 80

Special Note

Throughout this book you'll notice that the words
Personal Assistant are not abbreviated. The reason for
this is that in the entertainment world the PA is known as
a production assistant, and though the two positions hold
many similar challenges, they are very different positions.
This guide focuses on the many areas related only to that
of the Personal Assistant.

Also, you'll notice that I switch between using *her* and *him*
throughout the guide to indicate the employer.

At the end of this guide is information on how to
download the **templates** and **_forms_** that will help you to
get up and running fast, and enable you to perform your
job successfully.

Introduction

Who hasn't dreamed of soaring through the skies in a
private luxury jet, relaxing in a plush, soft leather seat that
engulfs and surrounds you while being served poached
salmon by a beautiful hostess at a thousand feet up?

Or imagine how cool it would be to have Carte Blanche
access to exclusive, A-list Hollywood events or rubbing
elbows with tomorrow's megastars?

Perhaps you've always wanted to be a liaison for the
world's foremost diplomats, scientists, researchers, heads
of States, or rulers of countries. You'd love nothing better
than to attend a United Nations conference, shake hands
with the President, or enjoy a front row seat while
watching Congress deliberate over a heated issue.

The dream is real. You can do all of this and more. In fact thousands of people do every day. They're not rich, don't have celebrity status, don't own a fancy house, and they don't even possess a large bank portfolio. So who are these people? They are the Personal Assistants who work for the rich, the famous, the tops in their fields, the crème de la crème.

The world of the Personal Assistant can be exciting and fast paced. It can take you through a hundred new experiences in a week and promises to always keep you challenged. The job can make you laugh and it can make you cry. Its addictive nature can thrill you, making you beg for more. It can also devastate you and make you wish you never even heard the words *Personal Assistant*.

This is a book about the very essence of being a Personal Assistant. In it you will find the tools, the experiences, and the secrets about the lives of this elite group. You will learn all you need to perform this job with confidence and success.

If you take the time and study the guide before you, it will teach you how to succeed in this amazingly frenetic but wonderful field that is fast becoming increasingly popular, highly sought after, and more respected with each passing year.

The tools you walk away with are ones you'll be able to use in almost any job and almost any situation. It doesn't take money or success, but it does take drive, smarts, confidence, ambition, and hard work to obtain a great job as a Personal Assistant. The opportunity is there for you to take, but you must want it or you'll never get it.

I challenge you to learn and take as much as you can from this handbook and do your best! Because once you see how exciting it can be, you may never want to work in another occupation, again.

Outlined in this guide are the tools and techniques for getting, doing, keeping, and excelling at an exciting career working as a successful Personal Assistant. And for those who already are working as Personal Assistants, there are useful sections inside that will increase your talents and secure your position in this field.

Employers will benefit by knowing who to hire and how to hire the right person for them, how to keep the best person, and never hire wrong again.

Part 1: History And Evolution Of The Personal Assistant

Chapter 1:
What Is A Personal Assistant?

You know about them, you've heard of them, but rarely will you ever see them. At least not the exceptional ones. They run in the circles of the rich and famous in a "Where's Waldo"-like fashion. They speak on a daily basis to the A-list celebrities, heads of State, creators of multi-million dollar corporations, sought-after lawyers, doctors in demand, top athletes, powerful executives, and brilliant entrepreneurs, yet you rarely ever take notice of them, or hear of their amazing deeds. These little known yet integral parts of our society have been around for many years. They go by the often ambiguous title of *Personal Assistant*.

Some think this term fits a wide range of jobs from secretary to runner to administrative assistant. In fact, because this job encompasses so many skills, employers often assume that anyone can fit the role of Personal Assistant. This is not the case. Most often the untrained person who is hired as the Personal Assistant gets so overwhelmed that they end up leaving, or is fired because they could not keep up with all the high-pressure demands. A good Personal Assistant can do a variety of unusual tasks that require experience, knowledge, and a drive to succeed.

Can a secretary, runner, aide, gofer, pa (production assistant) administrative assistant, nurse, or seamstress, become a Personal Assistant? Yes, perhaps. But it takes more than just the fundamentals of these job skills. There is a mental attitude that goes into the mix. Part is a desire to serve and help others. Part is to derive a satisfaction after completing a tough or challenging task. Part is a unique ability to jump headfirst into a new challenge or situation and be able to successfully get through it. Also important, are the abilities to work alone, unsupervised, and stay on top of things. The Personal Assistant can be part clairvoyant, part protector, part parent, and part caretaker. A good Personal Assistant must know how to drive any car, prepare meals on the fly, sew a button, be good with children, be a diplomat, know where to find a mean cup of coffee, or they may possess only some of these skills. Part of the draw is the excitement of being around power and money, but the bottom line is to always get the task completed - because however the results are accomplished, succeed or fail, it is always the Personal Assistant who is accountable.

How The Personal Assistant Came To Be

Many occupations have taken on titles that not only explain their function, but also help to define it. Secretaries slowly transformed into administrative assistants. Stenographers found themselves becoming court reporters. And runners became production assistants. Each of these new career titles gives the job a clearer identity, and helps to define its purpose. But what about the Personal Assistant?

One of the most ambiguous and misunderstood occupations, Personal Assistant has become a catch-all term for everything from the multi-tasking receptionist, gofer, administrative assistant or executive assistant. Look at the help wanted ads from people searching for a Personal Assistant. Most of them use descriptions that tell you the tasks are simple and imply that the person doing the hiring doesn't have time to take care of himself. They think they know what is expected of a Personal Assistant, but, in reality, have no idea what the position actually entails. The bottom line is that they are requiring *honed skills* and experience but offering *low pay* as compensation. They have no clue as to the skill-set that is required.

To most, the title of Personal Assistant fits any job description. Employers somehow latched onto the idea that if you do office work, and they throw in a personal errand every now and then (fetch coffee, pick-up dry cleaning, take the dog for a walk), that they can label you a "Personal Assistant." And this is where a lot of the confusion begins. Since a low paid runner or production assistant or mailroom person can do these things, then why should they be obligated to pay more for a skilled Personal Assistant?

Let's examine the difference between a production assistant and a Personal Assistant. By its very nature, the production assistant is usually a kid who is fresh out of college or is the son or daughter of a friend and is enticed by the "Hollywood" carrot being dangled in front of them by some executive who tells them that if they work hard and pay their dues they'll be rewarded with a great job in the future.

Very often, a beginning production assistant will have little or no experience, but they take this opportunity to get their foot in the door. It is how the entertainment business continues to draw people in for little or no pay. That doesn't mean that the production assistant isn't smart, in fact, a number of them have masters and college degrees, and again, this is their opportunity to break into an exciting field. However, production assistant is usually not their career job of choice and the low pay can often equate to minimal effort.

A Personal Assistant, however, is someone who usually comes to the table with some skills in one or two areas and is able to pick up other chores, yet never dropping the bigger responsibilities.

The Personal Assistant is not merely someone who fetches, they're able to multitask. They need to understand what they are fetching, and how best to fetch. But this is just one of many duties that will be required of them. Again, their job is to take care of the minutia so that their boss has the freedom to concentrate on work, home, or anything else important enough for them to need and hire the Personal Assistant. You are a master juggler, a supreme multi-tasker. Yes, most anyone can walk a dog, but can they do it while making sure the calls are handled, correspondence is typed, appointments are met, bills are paid, houses are managed, travel is arranged, and their favorite Grande double-latte is served up piping hot.

One of the earliest mentions of the Personal Assistant was in the film called "*All About Eve*" (1950). In the film, a young girl, Eve, is so infatuated with Broadway star Margo Channing, that she works her way into Margo's world and shortly thereafter becomes her Personal Assistant. Researching the history of the Personal Assistant uncovered that some of the first Personal Assistants were attached to film projects as production assistants, or they were actually stagehands, runners or often assistant secretaries – maybe even someone from the typing pool, who was assigned to attend to the needs of an actor or actress. Their job was to make sure that the actor or actress was "happy" while filming. This entailed everything from making sure they had their favorite drink, hobnobbed with other elite members of society, lived in the lap of luxury, or was protected from their own destructive habits. Working on a movie in the 40s and 50s they were assigned the task of sticking close to the star of a film and getting him/her whatever they desired to keep them happy during the shoot. There were also secretaries who were asked by their boss to pick up the dry cleaning or get lunch, or sometimes to escort a star or client to a social engagement.

What The Personal Assistant Is Today

Unlike the glorified secretaries of yesterday, today's Personal Assistant is so much more than a human dictation machine, coffee maker, or errand person. The Personal Assistant of today is someone who is smart, quick on his feet, resourceful, diplomatic, continually learns, is open to new experiences, and thrives on new challenges.

There's a movie that stars Anthony Hopkins entitled, "Remains of the Day" In it he plays a butler who is a seasoned professional at his position. His every move, every thought, and every fiber of his being is dedicated to the service of his employer. While you won't be expected to be this myopic, it's important that you understand that in order to be successful as a Personal Assistant, you need to be thinking about your every move. Much like playing chess, what you do today can have repercussions seven moves from now.

This is a fun and exciting field filled with adventure and Personal Assistants are often rewarded in surprising ways. And while it can be hard, sometimes overwhelming, and a constant challenge, it's never dull; it's a job that gives back as much as you put into it. You will come away with great knowledge, experience, solid contacts, and a proud feeling of accomplishment that you did your best at an amazingly difficult job.

The only thing that makes me sad about this field is that the Personal Assistants who work primarily for celebrities are usually the ones who are honored and recognized. There are however so many more Personal Assistants in less glamorous fields who are often overlooked, when more often than not they are nothing short of amazing in their role as Personal Assistants. This book is dedicated to them.

How This Book Can Help You Reach Your Goal

By the end of this book you will have been given all the tools needed to perform your job with confidence. You will be able to jump in and handle almost every situation you encounter. You'll know when and where to get the help you need to complete any task. You will become a valuable asset to your boss.

This book will teach you how to develop or enhance your skills to become a better Personal Assistant than you'd ever thought possible. And, you'll be surprised at how simple these steps are. In fact, you'll probably kick yourself when you discover how many of these skills and secrets you already possess.

You'll be shown every aspect of what a Personal Assistant needs to help him or her stay at the top of their game. Here is where you will find useful examples and tools that will make you invaluable to your boss. Using this guide will help you reach your peak.

Whether you've got the entertainment bug, you like working in the private or corporate sector, whether you're already a Personal Assistant, or even if you're just starting out, this book is written as a guide that you can use to help hone, perfect, develop, and understand the craft of the Personal Assistant.

Note to Employers

Employers will find this book useful too. If you're thinking about hiring a Personal Assistant to help you out, or you've had bad luck in the past hiring Personal Assistants that weren't right for you, this book will help you understand why that happens, and what to look for to ensure you have a great Personal Assistant. You'll learn how to successfully find, interview, and hire a Personal Assistant that best suits your needs and personality. It's often assumed that anyone can become a Personal Assistant, and for this reason alone there are many cases where a Personal Assistant didn't work out. Using this book, you will not only know how and where to find the Personal Assistant that's right for you, but you can be sure that they are ready to jump in and help you get things done.

As you can see, the Personal Assistant is always changing and growing. The different styles and various types of bosses that emerge dictate what new and unusual skills the Personal Assistant may need to acquire. And while there are always basic duties and recurring themes in our role as Personal Assistants, there's always some new task that has never been encountered before and will have to be learned and adapted to. Let's get started!

Chapter 2:
What's Going To Be Expected Of You

How Your Position Defines You

There is an unspoken rule that the Personal Assistant must recognize and always be aware of: "You are not hired to be, and may never become your boss's friend." This is the black hole of the Personal Assistant's universe. Yet like a moth drawn to a flame, this is where many Personal Assistants gravitate since it seems like such an inviting, open, welcoming area, because you will spend many hours in close proximity to your boss; joking, talking, sharing a story. It can seem like you are becoming fast friends. It's not that this can't happen, but almost always is the reason a job can end abruptly. While it's true that great friendships *have* been forged out of these working relationships, the exceptions are extremely rare. It's easy to see how this can happen since you spend so much time with your boss in close proximity and are often privy to very personal details they might share with you.

But it's important to remember not to get caught up in the social aspects of the job, and that the true role of the Personal Assistant is to cater to the needs of the employer – whatever that might be.

So what exactly is the role of the Personal Assistant? What function does she or he serve and where does she draw the line of unacceptable tasks?

The Personal Assistant can be many things to many people. Since you may be involved with both the home and the office, depending on the needs of the employer and the requirements of the job, duties can often overlap. The Personal Assistant becomes a trusted member of the household staff, handling all of the confidential responsibilities for the employer. Duties may include; hiring, training and supervising staff, making and scheduling appointments for the employer, taking charge of all correspondence to and from the employer, handling all travel arrangements and creating the itineraries, doing or assigning maintenance work to be done on the home(s), acting as a liaison, and any other personal requests the employer may make.

A Personal Assistant may also perform only secretarial responsibilities, i.e.: typing, emails, letters, memos, and thank you notes, taking dictation, proofing and transcribing important correspondence or business documents, answering the phone and taking messages, opening, sorting and/or answering mail, setting up and managing files for letters and other important documents, or any other kind of clerical work.

Though a number of employers do have business managers, the Personal Assistant may also be asked to act as bookkeeper and manage the family finances, track expenses, manage records for tax purposes, research and keep track of investments, or obtain quotes on major renovations of the home.

In today's world of fast-paced technology, the Personal Assistant needs to have excellent computer capabilities and will usually maintain extensive warranty and inventory files (e.g. **The Bible**, which we'll discuss in Chapter 17 – is also known as a *Household Management Reference Book* and, is an invaluable tool which anyone in the household can quickly reference to find answers fast.).

Or the Personal Assistant may be asked to travel with their employer and keep them company on a long arduous tour, journey, or business trip.

Whatever your job, you will begin to see a pattern emerge that will dictate what kind of Personal Assistant you are becoming. Who you report to, which staff members you interact with, whether you begin your day at their home or the office, you'll begin to understand if you're becoming a behind-the-scenes Personal Assistant or if you are becoming someone who needs to be at the wheel, taking charge of every task as it arises.

Don't Expect A Typical Day

You can plan, prepare, and anticipate what will happen tomorrow, and when you arrive you're told by your boss to cancel everything because he's going off to play golf for the day. In other words, there will be times when, no matter how meticulously you plan things can change on a dime. Breathe, exhale, and start rearranging the schedules. Often, you will find, that this is a roll-with-the-punches kind of job.

One of the most common tasks of a Personal Assistant is doing the personal shopping for the lady or gentleman of the house. Therefore you need to be aware that the shopping habits of the wealthy are very different from the average person's shopping habits. Whether it's for groceries, clothing, or gifts, a wealthy person has no problem spending large sums of money for their personal needs. They may tire of last year's car or want to add to their collection, or they may want to spend a million dollars on a wedding. You may therefore be asked to help design part of an estate, or locate a new home. You may not only plan the family vacation to the Four Seasons in

Punta Mita, Mexico, but also go along. You might handle dinner reservations at the premium restaurant in town, or listen to how their day went, or perhaps go grocery shopping for them. They may have you contact Vera Wang because they need a new dress for an awards show.

Now imagine the power of having access to someone's credit card, checking account, or petty cash, and finding yourself being sent to some of the most exclusive stores in town like, Barney's of New York, Dolce Gabbana, Prada, Neiman's or Saks; it can be very enticing to sneak an extra little item you think you deserve onto the shopping list. This is why it is so important for the employer to make sure that the person being hired is well screened, has signed a confidentiality agreement, and has undergone a thorough background check performed by a licensed private investigator, background service agency, or attorney. As a Personal Assistant, you'll be given a lot of financial freedom with someone else's money and it's imperative that not only do you have their trust, but that you do not take advantage of it once it's given.

So who typically hires a Personal Assistant? Here are the most likely people to use the services of a Personal Assistant:

Celebrities – To the general public this appears to be the most prevalent group of people who use Personal Assistants, but it only looks that way because celebs are always in the limelight.

Entrepreneurs – People who invest or invent or create and are always on the go and need someone to assist with their schedule to keep things in order.

Business Executives – Usually their Assistant is in the office but can also take on duties in the personal life of the employer.

Directors – Because they travel or are always on the set or in production, they have little time to manage their personal lives.

Athletes – Like entertainers, they travel a great deal and sometimes need assistance on the road, or assistance with the family while they are away.

Producers – Like the Director, they can be on location or in a busy office.

Authors/Writers – Keep up with their work as well as some personal chores.

Politicians – Mainly they have an Executive Assistant, but they also have a need for personal services.

Doctors – They have secretaries who help them, but some need help in their private lives as well since the demands of their job leaves them little time to attend to personal tasks.

Lawyers – Their hours are often long, so they can often be in need of additional help to keep their lives on track.

Real Estate Agents – They usually work on multiple listings and need someone to attend their schedule, field the calls, sit at an open house, handle correspondence, and also take care of the personal choirs; dry-cleaning, auto, groceries, etc.

Music professionals (Artists, Producers, Labels execs, etc.) – This is another group whose schedules are random and chaotic and they simply don't have the time to even think about something as simple as dinner or travel arrangements.

In essence, anyone who has the money, but not the time, inclination, or the ability to do the task for themselves can be in need of a Personal Assistant.

Demands Of The Job

The President of the United States has a Personal Assistant known as a *Body Man*. His job starts an hour or two before the President's and entails everything from carrying an overcoat for outdoor speeches, to the smallest of details. He knows that President Obama, likes MET-Rx chocolate roasted-peanut protein bars and bottles of a hard-to-find organic brew - Black Forest Berry Honest Tea. He keeps a supply of both on hand. He has a list of immediate contacts at his disposal, VP, doctors, White House attorney, etc. He knows when to stay in the shadows and when the President needs a well deserved break. And, he know how to keep the pressure on President Obama when he's controlling a basketball on the court.

Like the coveted *Body Man*, a good Personal Assistant is prepared. He knows how to organize for the coming day. He reviews everything on his agenda, then prepares his employer's day and schedule accordingly. He is aware of his entire world. Say for example, your employer is an Entrepreneur. You read the news daily and notice that there is a new merger happening with a company that he has been keeping an eye on. This information, along with who the players are, can be invaluable information to your boss. Or let's say that because you keep your boss' calendar, you may know the upcoming birthday of a friend or relative and you need to alert him about a party, or discuss purchasing an appropriate card or gift.

Seeing into the future is one of the many talents a good Personal Assistant possesses. And it's not hard to master. One of the ways to keep on top of things is through a laptop or PDA device, which allows you to program reminders for days, weeks, even years in advance, and then set alarms twelve days prior with a reminder notice that an event is coming up soon. This allows enough time to stay on top of every event without having to cram it all into your head. And this way you give my boss a good heads-up well in advance. This can include birthdays, annual charity events, award shows, upcoming travel, holidays, rent, bills (theirs and yours), anniversaries, etc.

Another useful tool is preparing a yearly calendar. Events may change or new ones may develop, but at least you'll have an overall view on everything that can occur with few or no last minute surprises.

A good Personal Assistant is also not afraid to get his hands dirty. You may be asked by an employer to call someone in to replace a screw, a light bulb, move furniture, buy flowers, change the oil in a car, fix the timer on the oven or VCR. It amazes them when a good Personal Assistant is able and willing to do these things his self. (It's rumored that Liza Minnelli was surprised that her assistant knew how to use an iron, wondering where she had learned it.) However, you only should do these things if you know how, and if it doesn't take away from something more pressing. Sometimes it's more important to outsource these tasks. We'll discuss when it's best to do so.

A good Personal Assistant can tackle a situation without any handholding. If your employer gets invited to an event at the last minute and doesn't have a clean suit, needs an appropriate gift, or needs an immediate appointment for hair or manicure, you need to be on it. Or maybe the charger on his cell phone breaks down (always keep one or two extra on hand). You'll look like a miracle worker when you have a replacement on hand for something that fails to work properly.

Sometimes a good Personal Assistant is merely a good listener. This important people skill is one few have mastered and takes some practice, and it can benefit both you and your boss if you can be supportive when she needs it.

New And Already In Demand

From the moment you are hired you may find yourself thrust into several important tasks. It's surprising how much trust you're given so early on in your new position. A lot of people think that you need endless hours of training to be a great Personal Assistant. While it always helps to improve your skill level and can only make you better at your job, you might not realize how much training and skill you already possess. For example, have you ever visited another city or country? Taken a CPR class? Are you organized? Have you ever put a bookcase together? Obviously you've shopped before. Are you computer, Internet or email savvy? Can you cook? How are you with children or pets? How are your phone and people skills? Do you enjoy driving? Do you know your way around the city you live in? If so, you may already have many of the skills required to be a good Personal Assistant.

So what about training? You might be someone who already travels a lot but has never flown on a private jet. There are ways you acquire the know-how on a particular subject. For instance, you can learn if there are luggage restrictions on private planes. Can a jet can take off or land in different kinds of weather? Are there limitations to the time of day a jet can fly? Where nearby alternate airfields are located. If dogs can fly on private jets and what are the regulations.

All this and more can be learned. Sometimes, you'll be thrown into a job and have to learn as you go, but the better prepared you are before hand, the easier you will make it for your employer. And this might be the difference between hiring you or someone else.

Understanding what's going to be expected of you can make the difference between doing a good job or a great one. It can also determine how much you enjoy your work and how long you survive in this business. Don't be afraid to ask questions. It shows a desire to learn, an ability to communicate, and it tells your boss that you're thinking about the job. The more you understand what's expected of you, the better prepared you'll be.

Chapter 3:
Can Anyone Become A Personal Assistant?

Yes. But it depends on your motivation. Are you in it for
the money? Does the possibility of world travel excite
you? Are you enamored with the film industry? Or are you
simply trying to get a leg up or use this to acquire new
skills or contacts?

What Is Your Background?

Do you have a desire to serve? Are you the kind of person
who likes to do volunteer work? The real answer can be
found in looking at your attitude. Do you, and can you put
other people first? Are you willing to possibly miss out on
things that matter to you?

Here are some examples of professions that feed nicely
into Personal Assisting

- Secretary – Office skills, diplomacy, organization, tact,
  resourceful
- Executive Assistant – Gatekeeper, guide, liaison, partner,
  right-hand
- Runner – Gofer, errand person, coordinator, assistant
- Newbie – Adaptable, enthusiastic, fresh, willing, energetic
- Student – Capable, learned, smart, savvy, eager
- Nurse – Caring, patient, tireless, nurturing, take charge
- Waiter – Prepared, alert, quick learner, endurance, friendly
- Actor – Quick study, personable, adaptable, jack-of-all
- Mother – Mature, sensible, experienced, wise, supportive

Another *important* thing to think about is how thick your
skin is. When you become a Personal Assistant you are
sometimes the closest thing to your boss, closer
sometimes than a spouse or family member. And often,
when things don't go her way, the frustration can rain

down on you. So the question is; "Can you handle things without taking them personally?"

You have to remember that number one, this is a job. It's not personal. Two, that your boss may not be mad specifically at you but at something else entirely. Thirdly, you have to be willing to do whatever it takes to help fix the problem. (Sometimes this isn't possible. It's true that there are some jerks out there who are always on a power trip, but that goes for any business, not just entertainment.). See the movie *Swimming With Sharks*, starring Kevin Spacey.

The funny thing is that most Personal Assistants are women who in general are more empathic than men. This can be both a good and bad thing. Women can (sometimes intuitively) sense what is going on. The problem is that they can also take too much to heart, so when their boss yells or is frustrated, the (female) Personal Assistant can take it too personally and begin to think it is her fault. Many Personal Assistants have shared their stories while crying that their employer hates them or constantly yells at them. This is especially prevalent in the entertainment business.

Do You Have What It Takes?

There are going to be many days and many employers who will beat down on you verbally and make everything your fault. There is actually an amusing book called; "It's All Your Fault!" about this phenomenon. There are going to be days when you'll find that no matter how carefully you've planned, how meticulous you are, or how good your intentions, something will go wrong and fingers will point at you. It is inevitable that at some time in your career as a Personal Assistant, someone is going to say or do something that will make you feel like the lowest common denominator. (One high-level T.V. executive does it just to keep her Assistant from developing any ego, and constantly berates the Assistant whether it's warranted or not.)

Still, women Personal Assistants aren't alone in this arena. There will be times where you cannot fix the problem. That doesn't mean you don't try everything in your power to resolve the situation.

Does This Job Suit Your Lifestyle?

Do you know what type of person you are? Are you someone who is close to your family? Do you spend every holiday, birthday, anniversary, and special occasion with loved ones? It's important to know as much about yourself upfront so there are no surprises in the near future. Since we understand that there is no typical day in the life of the Personal Assistant, you can also be assured that there is no typical lifestyle as well. There are Personal Assistants who travel *everywhere* with their boss. There are those who don't travel (perhaps a second Assistant), who work long hours, sometimes twelve to fourteen hours a day. And there are Personal Assistants who come home at the end of the day. They might be married, have a pet, or simply have done the 24/7 thing and want a more structured work environment. Dennis Hopper's Personal Assistant is someone who, before going to work for him, traveled everywhere at the drop of a hat. Her schedule was chaotic and she was always on the go, often missing important family or social get-togethers. After many years of living this kind of lifestyle, she decided to reexamine what her life was like and what was important to her. So, she began to seek out a Personal Assistant position that would allow her time to socialize and have more *personal* time.

What Kind Of Personal Assistant Do You Want To Be?

Are you someone who's adventurous? Are you a person who is meticulous and always crosses their t's and dots their i's? Do people say that you are a nurturing person? How about hands-on? Are you the type that gets in there and gets a job done?

When beginning to understand which direction you want to go in, it helps to understand where you are best suited. It's not enough to just say I love being on a movie set or attending a premier, because in reality, while you may be present at those events, it's very likely that you will be running around taking care of all the last minute details that somehow fell through the cracks. Watch or read *The Devil Wears Prada* if you think differently.

If you have decided that you want to work for an athlete, then your project is to figure out everything that working for one might entail. Most athletes travel frequently, they may have several houses in different cities, the better ones have multiple cars. Some have families and you might stay home while they travel to help take care of children or pets, or to meet with contractors while they are away. Or you may go with them and help coordinate their press and publicity schedules with the publicity agent. They may want you to set up their hotel room a particular way, or shop for special foods. Help them purchase clothing. They may have you handle all correspondence for them because they're busy at practice or preparing for a game. If you travel with them, you may very possibly be responsible for packing and unpacking, possibly ironing, dry cleaning, and occasionally sewing. You may have to act as gatekeeper for those who want to get close to your boss.

Once you decide what kind of Personal Assistant you want to be, your next step should be to research as much as possible to see if this is something you really want to pursue.

This is a very fun and exciting business but it's also all consuming, so you must do research and really decide if this is for you. Because once you commit, it's a roller coaster ride that can have some crazy twists and turns that you might not be prepared to handle. It's best to investigate and explore as much as you can about the kind of Personal Assistant you want to be. A good step towards understanding what direction you are suited for is to have a comprehensive analysis about the type of person you are. Two great sources for this are *Myers & Briggs or www.analyzemycareer.com.* Here you will find a number of aptitude, personality, and occupational tests whose results will tell you where your strengths lie and your weak spots are. It will help you to see clearly what types of occupations and employers you are best suited for.

Part 2: Secrets For Getting Hired

Of course the best way for getting hired is to have a referral or recommendation from a close friend or associate of the person seeking to hire the Personal Assistant. If you don't have these kinds of connections in your arsenal, then you will need to be resourceful in finding where the jobs are. You can be assured that by the time you find the position others have also found it, but the second part of getting hired is to stand out. In the next few pages, we'll discuss the *secrets* you can use to rise above the competition and how to make yourself look like the perfect selection for becoming their Personal Assistant.

Chapter 4:
Finding Where The Jobs Are

Agencies, headhunters, networking, word of mouth, special listings, the Internet, job sites, friends, family, and using your brain to find every place that could be a lead for a Personal Assisting position. There is even a technique using *Who Represents.com* that we will also go over.

Once you've figured out which area you want to work in (music, entertainment, politics, sports, etc.), you can begin outlining your search criteria.

One of the better places to begin is with the placement agencies. The good ones should not charge you a dime for registering with them. Inside is a list of the better agencies, but you should be leery of the ones who want to test you like they would a secretary. It is not often that you would have to take a typing, spelling, and math test like some placement agencies have their candidates do. If your agency is seasoned in placing Personal Assistants, then they should sit down with you and thoroughly go over and review your entire background. Remember, some of the Personal Assistant positions out there never do a single day of typing or filing. There are many that do, in fact a majority of them, but this is not the only criteria for getting the position. As you will read again and again throughout this guide, the things you will be hired for first and foremost are, if your personality is similar to your boss's, and that your skill set compliments the position. Your age, experience, and job longevity are also important but secondary to these.

Another source for job seeking are your connections. Word of mouth can sometimes lead to an opportunity you might never have heard about through conventional methods. You never know who knows whom. Your father may have a friend at work who just got an account with Shaq, and he just happens to be looking for a new Personal Assistant. You just never know. So put the word out. A lot.

Let's talk about back doors. Sometimes, especially when you are newer to this field, the doors all seem locked up tight. So how do you get in? One of the many things you'll learn in this guide is that when you are on the job, you must find creative and resourceful way to get a task done. So why shouldn't job hunting be just as creative?

You've heard this term many times before. Internet Hackers often use *back doors* to get into sites that are protected. So why shouldn't you use creative *back doors* to get closer to celebrities, or high-powered people who are also protected. You just have to know how to get in.

Let's say for example you are one of the many people who want to work within the entertainment business. It's a hard business to crack and very often you find that you have no allies. So how does one get close to the stars or the producers or directors?

One method is to do extra or background work. You will need to register with one of the agencies, pay a fee and take almost an entire day to get registered, but once you do, they will start calling you for various TV shows and movies. If you are lucky, you might work on a show for several days. The bad thing is that the pay is not great and the hours are long. The good thing is how fast you can meet people and create connections which potentially could get you're the kind of work you're really looking for.

As you spend your time on a set, get to know the higher-ups. The production people, the crew, even the producer's assistants. As you begin to build a rapport with them you can slowly let them know what your real goals are. Sometimes they will invite you to leave a resume with them as, periodically, they hear of a position opening here or there.

This same technique can be used in volunteer work. Again, depending on the type of Personal Assistant you want to be, a number of celebrities, athletes, and politicians volunteer their time to various projects and this is a great opportunity not only to give to your community, but to work alongside these people. I even know one woman who is now the Personal Assistant to a politician whom she met while working with Habitat for Homes.

Do you work for a florist who delivers to high-end people? Are you currently working in the mail room of an agency or PR firm who represent A-list clients? If you let them know your ambitions after you've proven what a loyal, hardworking, dedicated employee you are, chances are you could be recommended to one of the clients who needs a new Personal Assistant.

Again, any avenue or creative way that you can put yourself into a position where the opportunity is there to meet the right connections, then you should take full advantage of that back door.

This guide will also explain how to go directly to the hiring source – the person you want to work for without putting him or her off. You'll have simple techniques for approaching someone as a stranger and having them invite you to send your resume to them, willingly.

You will use the Internet as a source for your searches (more on this in a moment). You'll also use periodicals, placement agencies, friends and relatives, cold-calls, contractors, and networking. Any resources you can gather.

The Essential Handbook for Personal Assistants is not condoning running up to them and getting in their faces. This can backfire in so many ways, you can come off like a stalker, or weird, or pushy. But, if you do it in a subtle way, perhaps by making acquaintances with the charity staff and letting them know what you do, then perhaps they may hear of something and since they appreciate the volunteer efforts on your part, it is a good chance that they may pass along your resume or information. But first, you must ALWAYS show that you can be a hardworking, dependable volunteer.

Searching on the Internet can be a good tool to start with. You never know who is going to be doing the job posting; it could be the manager, the agent, a friend, the old assistant, a relative, or even a search firm. So yes, while hundreds of others may be seeing this same ad, you must take the opportunity to investigate because they may not want all the others, there might be something that stands out on your resume that tells them this person may be the one.

You can never be sure when someone will post a new ad, you should do your searches twice a day. Once around 10am (because that's when the databases of new information are usually uploaded, and again around 4pm. Okay, so by this time you're probably saying big deal I put in Personal Assistant and I get the same worthless junk everyone else is already seeing.

This may be true in some cases, but what we will learn here is how to maximize the Internet to tell you more about a job then the information the ad gives. Let's say that again; the ad you find about a particular position may not have enough information about the job, the people, or the company. This guide will give you some tips and show you some tricks that can often reveal a lot more information then they wanted you to know.

Why is this helpful? Because sometimes an ad may promise more than the job actually is, and by finding out deeper information, you can assess whether you really want to pursue that job or not. Or, the opposite can sometimes be true. An ad may give little information and turn out to be for a big, important person and they were afraid to divulge too much information.

So let's try some experiments. It's true that hundreds of people are going to come across some of the same results as you will find in your searches, but then again, some will not know how to search correctly. And just because you and someone else finds the same job lead, it's the rest of your package that makes the difference in who gets hired. Your resume, your experience, how you interview, your clothes, and your personality, all goes into the mix when someone is deciding whether or not to hire you.

Let's get started. For our example we'll use Google since many of the search engines use Google's database for some of their own searching. Type the words *Personal Assistant* and see what you get. At the top of the list you'll notice the first couple of results are those that pay to be listed there. After that, you are most likely to find sites that are trying to sell you something or get you to try some product. Not much help.

Now try it again and this time place quotation marks around the words "personal assistant" but this time let's also add some key words. You can try job, classified, celebrity, placement, job, position, actor, etc.

Try substituting words, such as help, hire, work, employment. Or try describing the area you want to work in, "personal assistant" AND "clothes design". Even better, let's use some examples from ads and take some key words to create a search criteria. Try typing the following into Google's search bar: "personal assistant" *savvy*, or try *organizing*, or *computer skills*. Notice now the different results you get. You'll still have to weed through a few irrelevant listings, but notice also that your search returns are richer and with closer results.

Now, let's say that there is a job that you find interesting on Craig's list or Monster or EntertainmentCareers.com or showbizdata.com. But the information is very limited. You may be surprised by all the information you can obtain from this cryptic job description. First, let's look at the ad itself. What are they looking for? Pay attention to the kinds of phrasing it uses and the descriptions. For example, does it use the word entertainer, or actor? Does it say athlete or sports personality? Grammy winner, or Grammy nominee? Do you get where this is going? The wording they use can indicate if the position is for a true working star or someone who was a star and is now a *personality*. You are welcome to apply for either but know what you are getting into. Approach every job interview with open eyes and do your homework.

The second thing to notice is if the ad says that the tasks are simple but they want you to have a bevy of skills; computer, internet research, errands, shopping, managing the household, and they are asking for a few years experience, you can be sure that they think the job is easy, but they have no clue as to what's involved.

Why do they have no clue? It could be a manager or a representative who is posting the ad and really doesn't know all the details and important aspects the job entails. Often a placement agency who doesn't typically place Personal Assistants will get one odd job thrown at them by a referral. Or, the last Personal Assistant could have been so good at the job, keeping the minutia from the employer that the employer actually thinks the job is easy.

The next thing to ALWAYS look for is the contact information. Did they leave a fax number or an email? If it's a fax, it can sometimes be easier to research a position based on the number.

Again, using Google you can type in the fax number using dashes or dots and then press search:

Try all three versions until you get the correct results
310-555-5555, 310.555.5555, (310)555-5555

Want a real example of this? Scroll down to the ICM Talent contact information below and cut-n-paste their fax number into the Google search bar and look at the results.

A good deal of the time you will find search results with a company name. If there's a contact name as well, even better. Why? Now you can go to their web site and see if there is a company directory. If not, you might still be able to get some research done. If there is only a first name, then it may be harder, but if the person listing the position has also put their last name, then the next immediate step is to figure out is how the company lists their emails.

Let's say for example the person, *Judy Blah*, is from the ICM Agency. You go to their web site and immediately look for the "contact us" page. The first thing you should try to find is how they list their email addresses. You'll definitely see that the end part says *@icmtalent.com*. But does the beginning part say *info@icmtalent.com*? Or, *Submission@icmtalent.com*? What now? The next step is to figure out how they enter a person's name on their email address. Because if you can figure this out, you now have a direct contact within their agency. The way to find this out can be simple.

Type in: *www.betterwhois.com*. Type in the web address for that company (in this case *www.icmtalent.com, or whatever follows the @ symbol*) and you will come up with a page that says reserved. Next, scroll down the page and click on the "more info" link. Now you can see their contact info? No big deal, right? But hey, the contact and administrator emails have the same last part *@icmtalent.com*. And, this time it has by their name:

Administrative Contact :
International Creative Mgmt
gchun@icmtalent.com
10250 Constellation Blvd.
Los Angeles, CA 90067
Phone: 310-550-4000
Fax: 999 999 9999

Technical Contact :
Chun, Greg
gchun@icmtalent.com
10250 Constellation Blvd
Century City, CA 90067
Phone: 310-550-4296
Fax: 310-550-4262

So now it's a good bet that ALL the company email addresses use a first initial and last name, just like Greg's email does. Great. Now, using this same logic, you can be assured that you may have the right email address for the *Judy Blah*, the person looking to fill the position. You can then email her directly. But there's still more information you can gather.

If you now type "ICM actors" in Google, you will eventually find some pages with names of clients, former clients, and some of their agents:

> ICM represents high-profile clients including Chris Rock, Halle Berry, and Beyonce Knowles. ICM also arranged financing for Oscar-nominated films such as "Gosford Park, Moulin Rouge," and "The Fellowship of the Ring." The agency has lost several star agents in recent years, along with big-name clients (including Cameron Diaz and Julia Roberts) to its competitors. ICM was formed in 1975 by the merger of Creative Management Associates and The International Famous Agency.

More good info. Using this new information, let's move on.

Next, let's go to (Who Represents) *www.whorepresents.com*. For this one, you may need to sign up for a subscription (about $9 a month). Here, if you type the Agent's name you will get a list of their clients. And vice-versa if you type in the Actor you'll get a list of their representatives.

Back to our ad searches. Let's say you found a job ad looking for a Personal Assistant to an "Older A-list actress." (For fun, type *older a-list actress* into Google's search engine and see what results you find.)

You can probably narrow it down based on the ad description: *"Older A-list actress looking for a Personal Assistant. Submit resume to info@icmtalent.com"* You can guess that it's not Michele Trackenberg or Megan Fox and assume it may be someone like Meryl Streep, Helen Mirren, or Dame Judi Dench. Go back to Google and type; *"Actresses at ICM"* in the search bar and look at the results.

After scrolling through and reviewing a few page results one page finds a list of actors and actresses at (*http://www.hertsbirdclub.org.uk/addylist.html*). After typing several actresses names into the *Who Represents* database, *Anjelica Huston* came up as an actress with ICM. Clicking on her name, you'll find her agent there is *Boaty Boatwright*.

With a little work, you can become a creative sleuth and start to read between the lines of the ads posted on the web. It will take a little ingenuity, and you may not always get it right, but you can begin to narrow down your searches. Who knows! You may come across another celebrity you hadn't thought about before. Use the agent's contact info to send a nice letter and resume, yes by snail-mail or email, and introduce yourself asking them to keep you on file for consideration should a position open up. Most likely, the email may go straight to the agent's assistant. So be open, candid and ask to be considered or kept in mind for something in the future.

You can then use your judgment, research, and resources of what you now know about these celebrities and determine if it is someone you'd like to work for. In your research you may also learn or have heard that a particular celebrity is either difficult or that they go through a lot of assistants. But don't rely on rumor alone because there will always be rumor; "This one's a psycho", "That one's hard to work for", "I've heard that one throws things". Yes, there are some bad bosses out there. In ANY business. But unless you have direct information about your potential employer, do not listen to conjecture and rumor or you could miss out on some really good opportunities.

When looking at a job ad, notice everything on the page. Notice the agencies and make note of their web sites and names because you will be contacting them. Search any blogs or forums that come up because someone could become a good lead. Perhaps someone is ranting on how they used to work for Cheryl Crow and that her manager, so & so is a real hard ass. But here's the KEY thing to focus on. Now you know who Cheryl Crow's manager is and you can look them up and contact them to see if they represent other clients who may be in need of a Personal Assistant.

Look at some ads on the Internet:

> "Entertainment executive is in need of a full time personal assistant. Person must be very peppy and energetic. Must be thick-skinned and able to anticipate needs. Must be savvy and hip since person will be booking travel arrangements, purchasing client gifts and organizing the social events calendar. Person must also have strong computer skills and a good phone demeanor since they will be doing some administrative work."

Whew! That is a lot of work! And look at the reward for all this hard work:

– Compensation: $380 per week –"

So let's break this down a little. First, the position requires someone full time. Needs to be peppy and energetic, which implies lots or work, lots of juggling, and someone who is a go-getter. Thick-skinned simply means a lot will rain down on you in the way of demands, possibly verbal abuse, and your ego will be constantly tested. Savvy and hip translate to knowing how to finagle the best upgrades on airlines, using your wits, good taste, and *savvy* to find the most unique and interesting gifts. On top of all that, they also want a strong executive assistant; computer skills, phone demeanor, calendaring, and administrative work.

Now in the real world, just being an administrative assistant who has none of the other requirements or skills can earn quite a bit more than this position is paying. Yet they're asking for five times the amount of work required. A reoccurring theme here will be jobs that entice you with promises of entry into a world you find glamorous; the entertainment business. Be careful here, tread lightly, and keep your eyes open. If you break down every job ad you come across, you'll soon be able to figure out what they really want and then you can determine if the compensation is fair for you.

Let's look at another one:

"Busy owner of a hip Venice design company seeks a personal assistant to help take care of life's pesky little chores. Looking for a quick learner who's *friendly*, *smart*, and *extremely organized*. The candidate must have his/her own car."

Responsibilities:
- Errands, including grocery shopping, picking up prescriptions, dry cleaning, carwash, etc.
- Occasional dog care, including taking the dog to groomer and vet (very wonderful and friendly dog)
- Paying household bills and maintaining Quicken accounts
- Coordinating household appointments, i.e. plumber, electrician, telephone company
- General household filing and organizational assistance

Requirements:
- Reliable car and valid California driver's license, insurance
- Must like dogs
- Excellent organizational, communication, and administrative skills
- Ability to prioritize and handle multiple projects
- Detail oriented & self-motivated
- Fluent in Microsoft Word and Internet
- Preferably knowledgeable in Quicken and online bill paying

– Compensation: $10hr. – "

Can you imagine asking for the moon yet paying the equivalent of a bus ride to downtown? Again they're asking for a lot of talent for very little in compensation. Think about it this way. One of the requirements is to have auto insurance. Can you really afford auto insurance on $10 an hour along with your other bills and obligations?

Again, they try to entice you with words like *hip, Venice design company.* In return they want *friendly, smart, and extremely organized.* There is also the subliminal message that a lot of these duties are occasional or even easy. Review this ad and try to break it down. Closely examine every requirement and responsibility and see if it's fair. Also, if you do think it is fair, the next thing to ask is; was there previous Personal Assistant, for how long, and why she left.

You've seen dozens of these ads seeking someone who is obviously required to have skills and is great at multitasking, yet the potential employer wants to pay less than what a dishwasher or busboy might make. Why?

Most likely it's because they never see the creative ways in which Personal Assistants get a task completed, nor have they witnessed the personal sacrifices, often giving up personal time (without extra pay) to get the dry cleaning to their boss, or proof important correspondence before the next morning. They don't see how you ran all over town to get a task completed, using every resource at your disposal to find the answers.

The problem stems from the fact that either they really don't know what to offer for these skills or they are lumping Personal Assistants in together with an errand runner. An inherent fault of the job of a good Personal Assistant is that the employer will never see all the hoops, all the ingenuity, and all the perseverance used to complete the task at hand.

In your searches you might see a resume of a Personal Assistant on the Internet. Contact that person and ask them questions about how they got started. Sometimes they're willing to give information and may give you some leads. People are usually helpful if you don't come off as too needy, or clingy. They will usually answer a few questions to help point you in the right direction.

Does this make sense to you? You need to use every resource you can to get all the leads you can. Finding a job is like dating. It's a numbers game and the more you put yourself out there, the more chances and opportunities you'll find.

Another door to try are the concierge services that do Personal Assistant work. See if you can volunteer your services to learn the ropes and perhaps they may have a client who wants to hire someone full-time. Again, use everything you can and every door you can open to get those leads.

Doing an Internship at a production company or agency is an excellent way to learn the ropes and have them get to know you. The process can be a slow but you will begin to build a network of contacts and leads, and more importantly, a good skill set.

Getting back to *WhoRepresents.com* you can search for a particular celebrity you fantasize about working for. Research who is representatives are, then craft a nice letter to each one and mail it to them asking them to consider you or keep you on file for the future. Again, here you are using every resource available.

If you are interested in working in Washington, send your resume to your local congressman asking him or her to submit your resume to the person you would like to apply to.

If you want to submit to a sports personality, research if there is a charity they are involved with and send a letter to them asking to have your resume forwarded.

Using resources is a numbers game and the broader your reach, the more chances you have to get noticed. Again, be creative, use every back door, and always think out of the box.

> **SECRET:** The UTA Job List is an industry job sheet that lists open industry positions. But you'll need a contact to get on their mailing (not me). If you have a friend or resource this is a good source for job leads.

Creating A Resume That Gets You Noticed

First rule: For every job you can expect hundreds of resumes to hit the desk of the perspective employer. So within these piles and piles of candidate's resumes, how do you get your resume to stand out?

Let's begin by looking at what will automatically disqualify you and put your resume right into the trash. The likely candidates for waste receptacle consideration are; colored resumes, scented paper, photos, resumes that are more than two pages long. If you can't say it in one to two pages, then you've lost their interest. While you may have seen some online postings that request a picture along with the resume, you can guarantee that the job has little or nothing to do with Personal Assisting, and if it does then it becomes a discrimination issue, and your boss will likely be someone who will hit on you. Plus, you'll never know if you got the job from experience or looks. Why is that bad you say? If you get a job based on your looks you can almost guarantee that your boss has ulterior motives and you need to be very careful and clear about what his intentions are. Do not fall for the "We work with such beautiful models and actors that we need someone who makes our office look beautiful." So just how many pretty faces does it take to get a cup of coffee? Or file a document? Come on, get real.

When reviewing a resume, employers look for experience, longevity (at the job), similar experience, meaning that you've worked in a similar field. So what if you are new and don't have much experience? This can be an interesting area. I can tell you that one of the reasons Noah Wylie from ER fame hired his Personal Assistant was based on the fact that on her resume she had a military background. For whatever reason, he liked that quality.

You never know what someone will hone in on and it's important to be honest and also list your abilities, especially if you don't have much experience. This doesn't work for every employer, though. But The good ones will read your resume and see if there are skills that are translatable to their job opening. Keep in mind that the less experience you have working as a Personal Assistant, the lower your beginning salary will be. See *Salary Guidelines* below. It could be anything that makes your resume jump out.

Something that got me noticed by some headhunters was that my resume had been created in a brochure format on cardstock. They called to ask who designed it and when I told them I had, they liked the fact that they could sell my computer design skills as one of my assets. The fact that I knew how to create a brochure like this impressed them. They'd call me and say that it was unique and it made me even more marketable. And while it did fly in the face of the no colors rules (some of the words were in color), you have to know when to take chances and when not to. With headhunters and placement agencies, this can *sometimes* be okay, but never with the employer himself.

Your resume should at least contain the following:
- Your name
- Your address
- One or two *working* contact phone numbers
- Work experience
- Dates of employment – to illustrate length of time
- Description of your duties
- Any education, special courses, or skills
- Job title for every position held
- If there is a page two, ALWAYS put your name and contact info at the top and also put next to it: [Page 2]

- Put your OBJECTIVE at the top, but list your education and other skill sets at the bottom

If you are someone who can't write objectively about yourself, a good source for writing a resume that really will stand out and give you that extra advantage is: *www.resumewriters.com.*

Your resume should be concise and to the point. Not too wordy. Your resume is not just a list of past jobs, it's about you. It should reflect your strengths and objectives.

Say something about your character; *"Hard working"*, *"Diligent"*, *"Great at Multi-tasking"*. These buzz words should not just appear as a bullet list on the page but they should be used in the body or description of the duties you performed for each position you list. Also, vary your descriptions. Don't just say "Duties included running errands, shopping, filing, overseeing contractors,..." then repeat it again. The next description should use different wording; "Responsibilities for employer and his family included walking the dog, picking up the children on time, shopping for groceries,..."

Have several friends or associates review your resume and give honest feedback. A great technique to improve how a resume stands out is to hold it in front of you, close your eyes for a moment, then open them and notice immediately what jumps out at you. Which part instantly caught your eye? Why? Was the type bold? Did you use a different font or size? Color? Or did it jump out at you because it was too long or too short? When looking at your resume pay attention to everything that your eyes focus on and determine if it's a positive or negative, then change it accordingly.

Avoid typos. If you do put an objective or goal at the top don't ramble. Use wording from the ad description of the "ideal candidate" throughout your resume. Use action words. Remember that your resume shows who you are and what you can do.

References: What Yours Say About You

When someone reads a reference letter they immediately look for several things. Why you left, what you did in your prior position, and why your old boss is writing this letter.

When someone is considering hiring you, they are taking a risk. Even if you pass the background check and other interview requirements, they still want to know more.

Reference letters are an excellent way to further open the door and create interest from the potential employer.

A reference letter states how valuable you were to the former employer but it should also include a few examples of what made you such an asset to them. What specifically you did to win their graces. It will also include the reason you are no longer, regrettably, at that position. This can be anything from both of you going in different directions, to the job ending, it was a trial basis, whatever the reason, make sure it wasn't ended on a bad note.

> **Secret:** Ask them to leave the date off the reference letter. You never know how long you may be job hunting.

If asked to provide phone numbers of personal references, make sure they are a combination of both personal and business, and that these people are going to give a believable, positive assessment of you and your work. It is important that you let these contacts know you will be using them as a reference. It is best to ask for their permission first.

Personal Assistant Organizations & Affiliations

I will get letters about this but most of these affiliations are overrated, they offer some benefits (courses, etc.), but sometimes they can be a deterrent if your potential employer learns that you are a member. Employers in the Entertainment industry can often be paranoid wondering if you may discuss them and their associates when you get together with fellow Personal Assistants. They may think you all sit around comparing notes. Though that is not the purpose of these organizations.

The purpose of these organizations is to be a support system and resource for their members. The idea behind this is wonderful but the execution is slightly faulty. There are millions of working Personal Assistants in the United States and even more in Europe who aren't eligible for membership to these celebrity Personal Assistant organizations.

Why not have a support system that *everyone* can benefit from? As it stands now, only an elite few who have worked for celebrities can reap the rewards of these organizations. Their brothers and sisters who've not worked for a celebrity are left out in the cold. And if you do belong to one organization you may not have access to the resources of the other organizations. Additionally, few people working as Personal Assistants meet the requirements which make them eligible to join. The requirement is to have worked for a celebrity for a specific amount of time (about two years) just to be considered.

There are many working Personal Assistant who've never been in one of these organizations and it has never hurt their career. However, the sad part is that this could really be a fantastic support system for everyone to help them do their jobs at peak performance.

So, should you join a Personal Assistant organization? Do you need one to land a job? Which ones are better?

There are several organizations for Personal Assistants, the problem again is that none of them work in conjunction with each other, which makes absolutely no sense. In a field where communication, support, and especially networking are so vital to be successful at this coveted position, you'd think that they'd all want to share information and as a single unit. Help strengthen the field.

So, should you join? The answer is perhaps. Remember, that getting hired is a *numbers* game and the more opportunities you have to find a job the better your chances are to land one. It also depends additionally on what you want from the organization. They may all have job postings but you might not yet qualify for membership. That being said, Here is a link to each of the Personal Assistant organizations and what they can do for you. here are a few you can research:

ACPA – Association of Celebrity Personal Assistants
http://www.celebrityassistants.org

KCC - Kerri Campos Consulting
http://www.kerricampos.com

NYCA – New York Celebrity Assistants
http://www.nycelebrityassistants.org

CPAI – Celebrity Personal Assistants, Inc.
http://www.celebritypersonalassistants.com

ACA – Association of Celebrity Assistants (UK)
http://www.aca-uk.com

Also:

Professional Domestic Services & Institute
http://www.housestaff.net

Personal Assistant Pro
http://www.personalassistantpro.com

Salary Guidelines

While you will see job postings for Personal Assistants that pay embarrassingly low salaries (between $6-$10 an hour), you will also see some that are (at the moment) out of your reach.

And though the low salary can sometimes be a fair compensation for the beginning Personal Assistant with little or no experience, it is by no means a standard. On the other hand, for an experienced Personal Assistant with several years under their belt, you can expect to see salaries ranging from $80,000 - $150,000 and on the rare best earned occasion, $200,000 and up.

The guide below is a base to give you reference for what can or should be expected for certain skill levels.

Salaries will also differ from field to field. An athlete may pay more for a Personal Assistant that a Real Estate agent might. A director may pay less that an A-list actor.

Part of your job will be to determine in the interview what skills they will need, which ones you can bring to the table and then negotiate a fair compensation. And while you don't want to miss an opportunity by demanding too much up front, you can negotiate your review and instead of a six month review you can ask for a three month or sixty days.

If you can, try not to discuss salary at this stage of the game. While it is good to have an idea of what they might be paying, during the interview you may learn that there is much more to position and if your skills are up to par the salary should reflect these additional job requirements.

If they want to you drive your car as part of your job, you can try and negotiate a stipends for that. For example, the going rate for mileage is .37¢. If, to get to the job you have to drive twenty-five miles there and twenty-five back every day, which comes to $18 per day, or $92 per week, you could negotiate an additional $360-400 per month (non-taxable) as compensation for wear and tear, thereby increasing your income.

There are also occasions where the employer had no idea what he or she should pay and ended up paying way above what the job really deserved. Christina Aguilera paid a fantastic salary for a Personal Assistant who was only her traveling companion, keeping her company on long concert tours.

There are other compensations such as meals that may be included but this should not be a negotiating sticking point. You have to remember that you're trying to get the job and if you are too much of a stickler on too many minor points, you may end up losing the job opportunity.

However, if you are required to travel you should not have to pay for your own meals.

A health plan may be offered which may be important to you as part of the negotiated fee.

This is a general guideline of what a Personal Assistant can expect to make based on skill set and the duties required. This guideline was created by Kerri Campos Consulting *www.KerriCampos.com.* (Note: At the time of this writing the state of our current economy may reflect salary changes that differ from the guideline presented here.)

Compensation refers to the weekly gross salary based on a 40-hour work week

Salaries refer to Los Angeles based positions. (Cost of living adjustment should be calculated based upon alternate locations)

Runner

Compensation	$350 - $500 (to start) $400 - $700 (potential) *Generally an hourly employee, paid for hours worked*
Supervision	Needs supervision & direction
Qualifications	Some high school No special training
Duties	Errands Light phones Misc. projects (as directed)

Entry Level Personal Assistant

Compensation	$500 - $600 (to start) $700 - $1000 (potential) *May be an hourly employee* *May have some benefits*
Supervision	Can maintain certain routines without supervision Could be a 2nd or 3rd assistant
Qualifications	Some experience in an office or home

Duties	Basic office skills Basic computer experience *(Including all duties as listed in the above job descriptions)* Mail Filing Ordering Letters Faxes Copies Higher phone volume Packing

Full Charge Personal Assistant

Compensation	$700 - $800 - w/ 1-2 years exp. (to start) $900 - $1000 - w/ 3-4 years exp. (to start) $1000 - $1200 - w/ 5+ years exp. (to start) $1000 - $1600 potential *Generally a salaried employee with benefits*
Supervision	Requires little supervision
Qualifications	Career choice professional Proficient in computers Can think ahead Able to anticipate Multi-tasker Some college
Duties	*(Including all duties as listed in the above job descriptions)* Works independently Travel arrangements Scheduling Some staff supervision Staff screening Event Coordination / party planning Wardrobe Supplies Moves Handles money Liaison with business management team Delegates duties Overall operation of office/home

Veteran Assistant / Estate Manager

Compensation	$1000 - $1400 - (to start) - (based on a 40 hour week) $1200 - $3500 potential w/ 5+ years exp.
Supervision	Fully independent
Qualifications	College degree(s) or specialized job training
Duties	*(Including all duties as listed in the above job descriptions)* Hires, trains and reviews staff More involved in business; review contracts; able to make related decisions Full responsibility for home and/or office Ensure complete protection and privacy Coordinate scheduling Payroll Accounts payable and receivable Insurance and inventories Manage resources Research and recommendations VIP treatment of people Crisis solver More business involvement - may be an executive or partner Set up and maintenance of office(s) and/or home(s) Implementation of systems and procedures
Additional Pay considerations	Live in Foreign language(s) Specialized training Length of time with current employer Years of overall service Longer hours Weekends On Call 24/ 7 Job combining (e.g. nanny, cook, driver, etc.) Travel (per diem)

Benefits	Holidays Vacations Sick days Medical/Dental/Vision Retirement Stock options Comp time Credits Bonuses
Perks	First class accommodations and travel Gifts Film, music or other credits Memorabilia Hand me downs Meals Use of corporate privileges Invitations to parties/premiers/screenings/events

Networking - A Must!

To get a great job, to be successful at your job, to keep your value, you have to network. It is and has always been one of the best ways to look for a position. True, it may take a while, but the bigger your network the better your chances. So just how does one network? There are several ways. One is to take advantage of your network of friends and family. Let as many people know what you're doing and see what happens. Plus, one day one of them may run into someone who knows someone (as mentioned earlier).

Another method is to seek out the advice of an already working Personal Assistant. Almost everybody is willing to give advice and if you don't come off as weird or creepy they may offer tips on job hunting. Then, if they feel you aren't going to constantly call and keep bugging them (generally making their lives miserable), you can ask if they would keep you in mind if they ever hear of a position opening up. Again, it may take a while to establish this kind of relationship, but you never know. The field can turn quickly and a position can open up in a flash. A new Athlete, actor, producer, congressman, can come along and not have anyone in place. This could turn out to be a good opportunity for you. Plus, if the Personal Assistant ever leaves their own position, there could be a time when *they* contact you.

Additionally, if you know a secretary, mailroom employee, delivery person, contractor, landscaper, or anyone else you can think of who may know of or work for someone that could use a Personal Assistant, then by all means, network! Be creative, think out of the box, and use every resource you can come up with.

The Interview

Are you a good fit? So they like your resume and cover letter and now they want to see you. Who will you be meeting with for the interview? This is an area that is riddled with minefields. sometimes to insulate themselves from wannabes and people who aren't right for the position, employers will often have a placement agency, business manager, lawyer, or former assistant do the initial interview to weed out the not-so-hot prospects. The problem is that some of these people doing the interview may not understand what a Personal Assistant is or actually does and may not know how to properly interview you.

There have been many placement agencies who've never placed a Personal Assistant before, and are approached by a new client looking to hire a Personal Assistant. And the agency had no clue what to do. They had no prior experience with placing a Personal Assistant before, and have no idea what the job really entails, except perhaps what they've heard in the media that the assistant does. But they take the search request because they are looking to get a fee. Guess they figure how hard could it be?

One example is of David Copperfield the famous illusionist whose team, according to the ad, was looking to hire a second Personal Assistant. His lawyer was handling the interviewing process and both he and the ad mentioned the travel, the excitement, how great Mr. Copperfield was. But during the interview process, when asking the right questions, it came out that what they were really looking for was someone to be in charge of selling the T-shirts and other souvenirs, and occasionally assist the already in place first Personal Assistant. Oh, and the travel that was mentioned? While Mr. Copperfield flew private, the would-be Personal Assistant would be flying ahead in a commercial, economy class plane ahead of the group to help set up the tables.

Be prepared to ask a lot of questions during the interview and don't let the limelight of your potential employer cloud your judgment.

So how do you make the interview work to your advantage? By listening and asking the right questions. Does the employer travel a lot? Do they eat out or does someone cook for them at home? Does he or she work out of an office or their home? Will there be children?

All of these are good questions to begin to draw out from the interviewer anything that might be expected of you.

It also shows the person interviewing you that you are interested and involved with the interview process.

Another excellent approach is listening and remaining quiet, letting the interviewer talk. if they ask if you can do a particular task that is required, acknowledge with a yes and try to give a brief example of how you might accomplish the task.

What To Wear

The big interview day is here. What's overdressed and what's too casual? Depending on the environment you will be working in, you should always remember a couple of rules: No jeans on the first interview, and don't overdress.

Okay, so just what should I wear? If you are being sent by an agency, you can ask your contact what might be appropriate. If you are a guy it's always recommended to wear a clean suit but no tie. The exception to this is if you are interviewing for a politician, attorney, or head of a corporation. Then you should wear a tie. Even if you get there and everyone, I mean everyone is wearing jeans and ripped t-shirts, you need to put a good foot forward. They will sometimes tell you that the dress here is casual, but they will appreciate that you were respectful enough to dress for an interview and not your first day of school.

For women, don't over accessorize. Don't try to be too flashy or to show how great your wardrobe is. Also it's important to remember that you never, ever want to outshine your future employer. So dress nice, it's ok to look good, but you don't have to bring out the Jimmy Choo's or the latest Vera Wang.

Make sure your nails are cleaned, your teeth are brushed and breath is fresh (a deal killer). Limit jewelry. Comb, brush, or style your hair. Press your clothes. Don't wear colors that are too flashy. IMPORTANT: Perfumes and colognes are deal breakers!! Time after time people have actually been let go for coming to work "stinky". Resist the urge to scent yourself. No gum, no low-cut blouses, no shirts flashing chest hair. When shaking hands be firm but not hard. Women, don't do that limp-fish handshake or wear you only offer your finger tips. Yikes. Again, this creeps people out. You don't need to shake like a guy, just learn to shake properly. Wear matching socks and polish or clean your shoes. Replace torn or worn shoe laces. No piercing or tattoo surprises. If you have stuff on your face or neck, let them know before you come in. Check facial hair and nose hair. Avoid too much eye shadow or lipstick. Extra long fingernails; creepy.

Who You'll Interview With

Most often you will be screened before you ever meet with the person you'll be working for. Depending on how your resume got to them, if you were sent by an agency, you may already have been screened and had a thorough background check performed. A background check is nothing to be afraid of, unless you have something to hide. If you have outstanding personal affairs which may encroach on your job or if you've had any money problems which could indicate a trust issue. Background checks can also reveal if you've had any convictions or are presently involved in a legal skirmish, which your boss does not want to become involved in later.

Again, it's most likely that you will be interviewed and screened by either the previous Personal Assistant, the business manager, attorney, or sometimes a close friend. If you are interviewed by a representative of a placement agency or a headhunter, it's likely that this is a

prescreening to see if you are even qualified for the
position.

If you are being submitted through an agency, or a
headhunter experienced in placing Personal Assistants,
you will likely go through a rigorous screening process
where they have already performed a background check
on you and had you fill out pages of paper work in
addition to going through their own interview process
before your name is ever submitted. The good news here
is that their screening process puts you higher up on the
interview ladder and you are going into the primary
interview with strong recommendations behind you.

Negotiating Your Contract

It's best to try and not talk about salary at this point, but
that doesn't mean that you shouldn't talk about all the
aspects of the roll and what will be required of you.

Work Hours – Will this job require regular hours or are there
variable hours including nights, weekends, or holidays? Does this job
require routine overtime work to meet deadlines? Consider the effect
the work hours will have on your personal life.

Growth Opportunities - Will this job give you a chance to grow
professionally through development opportunities? Does there seem
to be a good chance that you'll be able to move up in the organization
over time? You need to examine what types of opportunities you are
seeking from a job.

Job Duties - Does the job you've been offered interest you? Will it
challenge you, or will it bore you to tears? You'll likely be spending
many hours on the job, so you want that time to be stimulating and
fun.

Company Culture - What is this organization really like? Do the employees seem to like each other and work well together? You should be able to assess the culture from your interviews. If your gut keeps whispering words of warning to you, it's a very good idea to pay attention!

Your Boss - Do you have a sense of your ability to talk to your boss? Do you feel you can communicate with him or her? If you feel your boss is likely to be distant and unaccommodating, beware.

Location - Will you be working in a busy city even though your heart yearns to work in a smaller area? Will this new job force you to endure a long, daily commute? Will you need to relocate?

If you get a sense that they are interested in you they may press you for your salary requirements. This can be a tricky area to finesse, don't hesitate to ask if you can get back to them shortly. You can also ask what their review process is and how long after you are hired do they have a review of your performance. If they continue to press you about salary requirements, ask them what their salary range is that they had in mind and then give them a range for yourself, with the high part being slightly higher than you normally would say.

An important aspect of negotiating your contract is to really interview the people hiring you and learn everything that will be expected of you. Often when you find how just how much will be required of you, you're more likely to negotiate a better rate based on the amount of work and time needed from you. Questions like how many hours your are expected to work. Find out what a typical day will be like for you. Are you responsible for more than one person in the household or the office? Will you be supervising other employees? Again, asking questions will give you a better sense of how to negotiate your contract.

What you do not want to do is say yes to $40K, $50K, or even $60K, and find out after you've begun that your job is 24/7 and suddenly you are locked in with no room for negotiation. Salary negotiations are normally done after an interview, at the time you are offered a job. The appropriate time to negotiate is when a formal offer has been made. If the offer meets your needs, by all means accept it. Never negotiate just for the sake of negotiating. There's nothing wrong with asking for time to consider the offer or outright asking if the offer is negotiable. The interview process is not a one-way street. It's your job to ask the right questions and enough questions to determine what they expect of you.

Are You Ready To Leave Today?

You hired! And, your plane leaves in one hour. Are you ready? Is your passport in order? Bags packed? While it may not be likely that you'll have to leave immediately, it's also not unheard of. There are Personal Assistants who, once hired, were given a week, day, or even a few hours notice before they had to be ready to ship out. You never know when it's coming and since they do expect you to be prepared – as you are the new Personal Assistant - just how ready can you be?

Worst case scenario, if they really want you, they're probably likely to work with you but that doesn't mean at your leisure. They really may have to fly off that day for a concert or premier tour, book signing, or sporting event. You might have to race home, get all your stuff and then meet them at their destination later that day or the following morning. So you need to prepare. Get your passport ready before you even begin the interview process. If you have a pet, pre-arrange a sitter that you can trust. Also, arrange for your car, your mail, your bills, and anything else that is time sensitive to be handled while you are away.

Always Request A Confidentiality Agreement

Why is this important? You've probably heard of situations where the Personal Assistant stole money from their employer or went on a shopping spree with their boss's credit card, or wrote a tell-all book after they left the job. So it's assumed that since all these things occur, the employer will want a confidentiality agreement to protect them, right? But let's look at this another way.

Say your former employer is a real piece of work. Everyone he meets, everywhere he goes, everything he touches, is a bad experience. He doesn't care who gets hurt as long as he gets his way. Now obviously he's going to leave a trail of people talking poorly about him. Let's say that talk ends up in a newspaper, or the tabloids. Suddenly this high-profile, former employer is looking to sue everyone. Who might he go after first? Assume he'll want to attack those closest to him, that know all of his deep, dark secrets, or perhaps it's a jilted girlfriend or ex.

The point is, you don't want to be caught in the wake of his wrath and you need some way to insulate yourself from his revenge.

A confidentiality agreement is a great way to protect yourself since you are now an unlikely source to reveal any dirty laundry. And it is your duty to serve and protect your employer. You will have more access to his personal and business information than almost anyone else on the team. So a confidentiality agreement is also a good way to remind you of the important and sensitive responsibilities that will be handed to you.

When to Ask For a Raise

You've been keeping track of all your long hours, all the over time, all the extra *above and beyond the call of duty* tasks that you've had to endure for the sake of your job. You've literally gone above and beyond what is required of you and you're beginning to feel the need for a little compensation. Especially when you see how easy and often your employer throws money around to everyone except you.

When you were first hired you did negotiate a raise up front, didn't you? No? You're probably wondering; How can you ask for a raise when you're first hired? Go back and reread the section on reviews. As a new hire you aren't going to ask for a raise, but you do need to have a conversation in the beginning about the review period. once it's apparent that they want to hire you, you should discuss a review period. Typically this can happen after ninety days or six months after you begin work. But again, if you are a good negotiator you can request a thirty or sixty day review.

A good negotiator who has several quality years working as a Personal Assistant can ask for a thirty or sixty day review. But if you don't have the conversation when you're first hired, it will be difficult, challenging, and uncomfortable to bring it up later. It's best if you document your scheduled review on a piece of paper preferably signed by both parties, just in case it slips the employer's mind when it's time for the review. Just like your confidentiality agreement, you want to have a copy of a review document stating when the review will be signed by both you and your employer or his representative (e.g. Business Manager or Attorney). Keep a copy of any and all documentation that you sign. People will forget things. No matter how great or nice your boss is even the best people in the world can forget their agreement with you. This is simply a reminder. However great your relationship is, it's still just business.

What If They Aren't Sticking To The Agreement?

Try as you might, prepared as you are, up front a person as you possibly could be, with candor and tact in addressing your needs, your boss has taken advantage of you and is not keeping up with his or her part of their agreement.

Was the agreement a promise that you'd be home by six? Or that you wouldn't have to clean the cat's litter box? Was it regarding a wage increase review? Maybe you don't do dictation and now they're upset? How about your benefits haven't kicked in or maybe the pay check is late.

There are times when you will need to speak to the business manager about these issues and there will be times when you need to speak directly to your boss. Whatever the case, you need to be tactful, calm, articulate, and prepared. Don't hem and haw. And never attack them. Try to pick a time to talk when your employer is in a good mood and not overwhelmed by affairs of the day.

You might be surprised to learn that your conversation jogs their memory and it was merely an oversight on their part, and things get resolved immediately. While most people do not like confrontation, ultimately, it can turn out to be a good thing that you came to speak with them about your concerns. Again, showing them your value by staying on top of things, being efficient and organized will help to bolster your cause.

Part 3: Becoming A Kickass Personal Assistant

Chapter 5:
Killer Techniques For Making Yourself Invaluable!

Congratulations! Or if you're already working, glad to see you're still working! Okay, this chapter will take you through what you will need to understand to begin your job. You will be given a guided tour of what will be expected from the very first day, all about understanding your role, and what should be known by you to help you excel at your position. The key here is to keep in mind that you are part of a team. Whether it's just you and your boss, or a whole staff behind you, all the other contractors, vendors, consultants, business associates, family and friends are already part of your boss's team and you are kind of like the assistant coach. Your boss will give you the general scrimmage, but it's up to you to see that all the team members – so to speak, carry out the play and make your boss proud of the results. Remember, your team may not always win, you may fumble the ball sometimes, and there will be times when you feel like you are being benched. But there are also the wins, the team victories, and the better prepared you are, the more practice and experience you get under your belt, the more successes you are going to have. So, enough with the sports analogies and on with the journey.

Understanding Your Role

You are the point person. Very often you are and will be the most direct contact to your boss. You will be expected to check in daily, prepared with the day's agenda, and make sure your boss is apprised of any and all meetings, calls, projects, and scheduling. You may be asked to be quiet as a mouse and remain in the background until called. Still, that doesn't mean you shouldn't be prepared when called upon. And while you are being quiet, you can and should have a lot to do. You should know what the day's schedule is like, what the week holds in store, both in business and personal dealings. You need to know where things are and who's who. You'll want to familiarize yourself with habits, routines, and anything else that your boss now expects you to know.

Your First Day

The first day can be different for so many people. There is a chance that someone who preceded you will be there to acclimate and train you. Then again, there may not. You may show up and the first thing in the morning, you'll be asked to get (important) so and so on the phone. Or you may be sent to get their favorite coffee. You may be nervous your first day and rightly so, but one of the key things to remember is don't be afraid to ask questions. Until you get used to things, you can't be expected to know how your employer thinks. So if she asks you for a tall cappuccino, ask questions. Decaf or regular? Do you take sweetener? Any special way? Extra hot, extra foam? Do you want a scone or muffin?

Don't stand there and have a five minute conversation either, just ask, write it down, and go. Your job is to get the information succinctly, and get the task done.

You Are the Gatekeeper

Part of your job will also be to protect and be a buffer for your boss. This role may make you the bad guy or the heavy to outsiders, but the key here is to screen and not let anything through that could possibly annoy, disrupt, or disturb your boss. Remember, you are there to help her do whatever she does best. And because she is successful at it, she can afford to have you assist her. So one of your jobs is to screen calls. To do this you need to learn who you should screen, when to screen them, and whom to let through. You can keep a list that has A people, B people, and C people. See the section on *Keeping Good Records* in Chapter 6.

Another role of the gatekeeper is to know the schedule. You are responsible for knowing where your boss is at all times in case an A or B person needs to get hold of her. As the gatekeeper you may have to roll calls, conference calls, take dictation, set up meetings, and return calls. As gatekeeper your job is to also limit unnecessary, potentially wasteful interruptions and unexpected interference that may negatively impact your boss's workflow or productivity. Any unsolicited, meaning uninvited inquiry, requires screening.

Basically, your boss is the queen of England and you're her guard. Nothing gets past you without specific approval from the Queen.

Having The Right Tools

Just what are the right tools for doing your job? It's different for each employer. Remember President Obama's *Body Man?* If you're traveling, your tool of the trade could be a messenger bag with many travel items, gum, water, pens, pencils, tickets, phones, batteries, ear plugs, band aids, aspirin. If you are an office employee perhaps it is a pad and pencil, a calendar of events and scheduling. If you're on set, a copy of the script, water, your boss's cell phone, a favorite food item. The right tool could be a computer, fax machine, Palm or PDA. The right tool for the right job.

Know your arena. By knowing who you are working for, and what's required of you, you'll quickly get a sense of the needs of the job and what you must have to provide good assistance. Again, in the beginning, don't be afraid to ask questions. This is one of your first important tools to acquire. Ask, be brief, listen, and always observe.

Knowing All The Players

A big part of your job will be keeping up and keeping track of who the players are. Your boss may have a big entourage or a small household staff. You will be interacting with most of these people on your boss's behalf and it's good to know who they are and what they do.

The *Business Manager* is responsible for most everything financial for your boss. He can keep track of payroll, big purchases, expenses, petty cash, financial contracts, household properties, taxes and more.

The *Attorney* is involved with all contracts, legal negotiations, sometimes investments and purchases, and again there could be financial endeavors which he handles as well.

The *Agent* handles meetings, appointments, contract negotiations, and anything involving career and career moves.

The *Press Agent* or *Publicist* deals with everything media. They are responsible for any and all public events which means that if your boss is attending a public event for publicity, there is a very good chance one of their reps will attend alongside your boss. You may be there too, but they will be responsible for knowing when to move him along and watch his back for potential media opportunities or paparazzi trouble.

The *Manager* is the one who puts all the people together. They help to open the doors of your boss's career, they check in with the agent to make sure your boss is being handled and shopped properly, that she is making good career choices.

The Players can also be people in your employers field that he has never met or worked with yet knows of. It's good to learn some about these people.

Watching The Clock?

One of the quickest ways to know this isn't the business for you is to take notice of how often you check your watch or the clock on the wall. This is a job that goes beyond time. This is the quantum arena of positions. Time is different here and like most people in the entertainment business can tell you, the day is done when the day is done. Some of you will be lucky and have a structured nine to five lifestyle, but most will not. It all comes down to getting the job done.

What Will Be Expected Of You

Remember way back when, someone at some time asked you what you wanted to be when you grow up? Was your answer "everything"? This is the kind of job where your boss may not know all about your background and experience, but will surely want you to know how to get something done when he asks. See the section heading; *You're Expected To Know Everything* in Chapter 6 for more details.

Know the Team

No matter how big or small the staff is you must be able to work with them. Even if your boss doesn't have anyone but you, there is still a team. This can include the travel agent, the phone company, auto service, dry cleaner, the gardener, pool man, delivery, etc. You are representing your employer when you interact with any of these people and you must know how to work well with them to get the best results. Ultimately, if something goes wrong or someone is upset, it reflects badly on your boss.

If there is already a staff in place it's often good to defer to the staff members since they know your boss's habits best and can provide you with some good insights until you learn the ropes. You are still ultimately responsible for how things turn out so while you can't give all the power away, you can use their work history with your employer to see how things have gone in the past.

If you will be working with a team you must keep in mind that they are there for a reason and have a specific task. You must never demean them and when you are asking for something from them on behalf of your boss. They can make or break you. This means they can make the outcome difficult or easy. Of course they too work for your employer, but how you treat them and handle them can determine how well they will work with you. And remember, you are the new kid on the block. They already know the ropes.

On a different note, an unspoken part of your responsibility is to get the best out of the team. If you are demeaning, rude, condescending, or annoying, they are not very likely to help out, and they may even drag a task out to frustration. You need to become a diplomat and show that you are a team player and that you respect and appreciate their job, and duties. Again, the players are also staff members. Think of the players as players on a basketball team. Everyone has a job to perform. Learn to be a team player and get to know your teammates.

Be Punctual

Another important criteria of a good Personal Assistant is to be on time. This is simple; you are being paid to be there. Whatever the excuse, it is just that, an excuse. Figure it out and find a way to not let it affect your job. You have been given a rare opportunity to really have an exciting job and career opportunity. If you are a compulsive over-sleeper, get over it. If your car breaks down, get a cab and call on your way there. Deal with the ramifications later. But never be late. Yes, for those of you who have to whine right now and find the one exception to this rule (family medical problem, or whatever), I can safely say that you will always look for these excuses and this disqualifies you from ever being a good Personal Assistant. Just as important, don't be too early either. Especially if you are working in someone's home. They may want and covet their private time so be respectful.

Chapter 6:
Preparing And Looking Like A Pro

At some point in your career almost everything will be thrown at you. You will have some challenges you can handle with ease, perhaps because it is something you've encountered before, and there will be some challenges that will give you a run for your money.

The trick is to prepare for anything that arises. I'm sure you're saying; "Easy enough said…" The best way to prepare is to visualize the position. Actually visualize it. Picture the place you'll be working, the surroundings. Once you've figured out what type of Personal Assistant you will be, then you can prepare. Example, let's say a part of your job is the grocery shopping. The easiest way to look like a pro here is to go through the entire fridge and pantry and make a list of absolutely everything. Once you have this list you can type it up and print it out. Put a check box next to each item and then you can do one of several things. You can post the list somewhere and let the family members check off an item when it is getting low or is out. You can go through the kitchen periodically check things off yourself. You can make a project for the kids to help you out. If there is a chef, check with him or her about their needs as well and add that to the list.

You can incorporate this same technique with many aspects of the household; office supplies, household items, Kleenex, parking change, sunglasses, toilet Paper, toothpaste, cleaning supplies, and more.

By visualizing your job you can add value by anticipating needs and tasks which may arise. Another technique is to get to know the other employees and ask them what your employer likes and what are his preferences. This can also give you greater insight into his habits and behaviors.

Are You Ready?

Being set for a position is being prepared. This can mean, researching your new boss, interviewing the person you are replacing and perhaps talking with some of the team to know what's expected.

You will need to know how to dress, where to park, and what time to arrive. If you can have his favorite morning beverage or breakfast ready, so much the better.

Carry a notepad and pen at all times. Simple things like wearing a watch, knowing the weather for that week, carrying a pen knife, tiny flashlight, a small sewing kit. Whatever. Be prepared.

Can You Juggle?

Your very first day you can have several things thrown at you at once. You arrive thinking that you'll be going over the daily schedule and you come in the house only to find out that your boss needs a ride to an appointment in ten minutes, then you have to pick up a last minute wedding gift, have a rip in his suit jacket repaired and pick him up from his meeting.

Can you do this while scheduling his travel, making luncheon reservations, and getting a stock quote? You will need to be able to handle everything that is thrown at you. If not, you need to rethink this field as a career for you.

Don't think you'll ever be in this situation? So your task is simply picking up the kids from school. What if just before you leave the house to pick them up, the pipes break and water is pouring into the master bedroom (See Chapter 17 on *The Bible* for tips on how to quickly handle this). Try having to pick up the kids from school and dealing with this at the same time.

Can it be done? Yes. Will it be easy? Of course not. Will your boss flip out? Maybe. But this will all be part of how well you can juggle.

Staying On Top Of It All

One of the most important things to keep in mind is that you can never let things overwhelm you. By planning and preparing, you can keep on top of your duties. There will always be something that can throw a wrench in the works as we just discussed, but if you review and keep up with your list of tasks, you can handle most surprises that come your way.

Try not to keep everything in your head. If someone calls you and requests something of you or changes an appointment, write it down then and there. This helps you two ways. Writing it keeps it better affixed into your memory and, you've written it down, which will allow you to add it to your task list.

Clothing

Always dress nice. This doesn't necessarily mean a suit or nice dress, but it does mean having clean, nice smelling clothes. If you smoke they will smell it. Keep your outfit simple but contemporary. Try not to outshine your boss especially if she or he is someone who is always in the limelight such as an actor or high profile personality.

It's also good to have some back-up clothes with you. This could mean a second outfit if your first one gets a tear or spill on it. It may be that you have to work late and are being taken to a dinner or public event. It's always good to have a black blazer or simple but contemporary black dress and some nice but comfortable shoes that look good in the evening. Black is always simple and doesn't make you stand out too much, but still allows you to fit in.

As in the rules for the job interview (this bears repeating) make sure your nails are cleaned, your teeth are brushed and breath is fresh (a deal killer). Limit jewelry. Comb, brush, or style your hair. Press your clothes. Don't wear colors that are too flashy. IMPORTANT: Perfumes and colognes are deal breakers!! Time after time people have actually been let go for coming to work "stinky". Resist the urge to scent yourself. Watch gum popping or chewing, no low-cut blouses, no shirts flashing chest hair. Wear matching socks and polish or clean your shoes. Replace torn or worn shoe laces. No piercing or tattoo surprises (unless okayed). Check facial hair and nose hair. Avoid too much eye shadow, lipstick, or extra long fingernails.

> **SECRET:** Always, always, always have comfortable shoes. You're never going to know how long you'll be on your feet, how much walking you will do, how much climbing, lifting, carrying you will be asked to do. So comfort is going to be your saving grace. But DO NOT come to work in ugh-boots or fuzzy slippers!

Electronics

If you are not gadget savvy, learn. Find a friend, salesperson, or neighbor who can show you how to use a piece of electronics that your boss uses. If there is a particular software program they use, learn it. If you are uncomfortable using a mouse, practice. Know how to sync a palm, update a Blackberry, and beam a contact.

You should know how to work ANY cell phone or learn fast. You need to be able to sync a Bluetooth phone to a car, work the stereo, navigation system, or even how to adjust the driver's seat. Simple? Perhaps. But it can and will be asked of you at some point. Remember, you are an employee and not a buddy. Your boss does not want to hear you say, "Yeah, I have problems adjusting my driver's seat too."

Learn what devices they use and learn the basics of how to work them. It is also important to know a technician that can tech support the devices should they malfunction.

How to Handle:

- **Production**

Here are some basic tools to knowing production. You should know how to keep and maintain your boss's files while on location or on set. Learn the system and who the members of the crew are; Director, 1st AD, 2nd AD, Production Manager, Line Producer, Writers, etc. Know how to find things in a heartbeat; contracts, scripts, NDAs, permits, releases, etc. Have your call logs prepared every day. Know the contact sheets and make sure you have a revised copy at the end of each day. Have a three ring notebook with the current script and any changes (page and script changes are usually notated with a different color paper to keep track of the last update or rewrite). Build a relationship with the caterer and craft service people. Also, know your surroundings; stores, pharmacies, gas stations, restaurants, clothing stores, hotels, etc.

- ### Premiers

When your boss attends a premier, if he is an actor he may have a PR rep to escort them down the carpet. If not, you will have to keep an eye out for news, media, and photo ops, and know who is looking to meet with them. If you know names, you may be required to whisper them to your boss. He may also be asked to do what's referred to as *Step & Repeat*, which means standing in front of a banner filled with sponsor logos while the paparazzi takes photos. Acknowledging fans is also important. You are like their guide dog, and you must look out for them and try to anticipate everything that will come their way.

It also can be as simple as keeping a sharpie (black or silver pen) on you for signing autographs (have a couple on hand). Having their sunglasses if it is still light out. Being able to get them water fast. Knowing where to go. Carrying wet wipes.

- ### Meetings

Will this be a dining meeting or not? Will drinks be required; water, sodas, etc. Is catering required? Do they have pens and notepad? Does your boss have all his files and documents? Is there a phone for conferencing? Do they have all the proper phone numbers and conference access codes? Will they need a special line for long-distance calls?

Do the guests need validation? Is there a Xerox machine nearby, a hole punch? A video monitor? Computer and DSL hookups?

Make sure there is plenty of time in between meetings for your boss to prepare, unless she or he specifically says that they want back to back meetings. Don't argue this point with them as they know best how they like to work.

Have any and all papers and documents, notes and numbers that they will need to prepare them for the meeting.

- **Rolling Calls**

Your boss is out and about. Can you get the call to him while he's out? If you are out you may receive a call and need to get an important call through to him. Can you forward a call from where you are? Are you able to listen in and take notes if needed?

The term 'rolling call' can be best described as follows: If you receive a call from your boss and he in turn makes you call other people, while he and you are still in conversation. In such cases you put both, your boss and the person he has made you call on a conference call. However you too will have to be on the call until the call is complete and then follow up with the conversation after your boss has finished.

One might face problems when there are other calls coming in during a rolling call. In such a situation, you are expected to put the conference call on hold and deal with the incoming call. But it has to be fast enough before the conference call gets disconnected. Some phones nowadays allow you to put the other two on hold without disrupting while you handle other incoming calls, and then you can return to the rolled call without any interruptions or delays.

▪ Messages

This is a very important area. You must keep good notes on messages you take. Time, date, person, alternate contact numbers, and, specific notes about the call. Try to anticipate questions your boss may have about the call and if you are comfortable, ask some of them yourself. "Is this the best number for him to reach you?" "Can he call you next week?"

Also, if you can, keep a detailed call log to reference so you can follow up on any missed or incomplete calls. There is a sample Call-Log included with the attachments for this guide.

▪ Recapping the Day's Events

Some employers may want a recap of the day's events. This can also include things that didn't get handled or even a sub list of what to expect for tomorrow. This also helps to keep you on track.

▪ Scheduling

This is never a perfect arena. Your boss's schedule could change several times throughout the day. You could plan for an upcoming event and at the last minute find out he will be playing golf that day and you need to reschedule it all.

Another part of scheduling is to try and give your boss some breathing room. Try to space things out, or if your boss is willing, try to schedule his week so he ends up having one or two "free" days.

- ### Errands

Try to coordinate your errands with your boss being out; shopping, dry cleaning, the bank. This may sound anal, but if you can map out your errands and put them in order so you use the least amount of time, this can help you get more done in case something comes up which changes your days plans. Make sure that wherever you are you can be easily reached. while you are out and about make sure you have the day's schedule with you at all times as well as any contacts or information you make be asked to provide.

- ### Driving

Be comfortable with driving a variety of cars. Simple things like how to operate power windows and the stereo can be important. Know the city you are going to be in. There will be times when a surprise errand will arise and you may need to know the closest fast food place, drug store, shoe repair, or gas station.

If you are driving your boss or his family or associates, stay calm, drive with the flow of traffic. If you are typically a honker, resist the urge. You don't want to do anything that will cause your boss, his family, or his associates any discomfort or anxiety.

If someone cuts you off, let them. Always make sure you are prepared and of you know you will be driving that day, make sure the car is gassed, and clean. Periodically check the oil, window washer fluid, tire pressure, spare, jack, etc.

If you have auto club, work it out with your boss that if you are going to be a regular driver that they should pick up that tab. Keep your own auto insurance current. If you drive their vehicles they may put you on their policy, but you'll still need your own insurance for your car.

Do you know that if you have your boss's permission, you are legally allowed to drive their cars? But check with the state you are in for the specific rules and regulations.

If you employer has a driver or uses a service make sure you know names and cell phone numbers. Keep in close contact and give them as much advanced notice as possible so they have time to wash and gas the vehicle and prepare any beverages or foods as required.

▪ Friends and Family

Learn who friends and family members are as soon as you can as you will be likely to be contacted by them. It's helpful to begin a list that you keep with notes about each person; birthdays, numbers, addresses, family members, etc. Keep collecting and gathering as much info as possible. You never know when it can be of good use. Always treat everyone with courtesy and respect, even if it is not returned in kind.

▪ Shopping/Returning

Keep a file of purchases and receipts. You might want to keep a notebook with Xeroxed copies or a file with receipts readily available. Sometimes your boss may lose or break something and want an exact replacement. It's also good to know where you purchased the item.

Keeping Good Records:

Taxes, auto records, children's school testing, home repairs, purchases and more. This is all a small part of keeping good records. At the time you'll least expect, you will be asked to find a legal file, a transcript, an old screenplay, or the kid's medical history. It is a good idea to have the files in a neat, logical and easy to find order. If you leave tomorrow, the person replacing you should be able to come in and find the files because they are easily and simply organized. Instead of having a file for every appliance, toy, computer, and shoe purchased, simply put them under a larger files labeled "*purchases*", and another under "*Home Appliances*", "*Auto*", "*Computers*", etc.

Then under each you can sub-label the manila folders, i.e. under the main category of "**Auto**" you can have a sub-folder for; "*Mercedes*", "*BMW*", "*Insurance*", "*Servicing*", "*Auto Club*", etc.

- **Files**

Make sure that your files are neat, legible and in logical order, so that ANYONE can find a file or document. Keep in mind that if you are not there, anyone should be able to locate a record. This also saves you from having to rush to the office when something is needed. And it will be simple to locate.

- **Records**

Keep any notes, updates, or changes together with the records. Always put the most current date on any updates. If these records are something that needs updating, keep a reminder in your palm about this item. Example: If you spoke with someone about health insurance, write a note directly on the file folder with their name, the date, contact info, and briefly what was said. If you've updated a warranty, make sure you have all the updated information, contract numbers, and service numbers.

- **Documents**

Create a filing system that allows you to quickly find a document and depending on the importance of the document, you may want to keep a log that has immediate information reflecting what is in the document, including, date, title, and summary.

- **Private Info**

Any private info must be protected. If you need to keep information with you make sure it cannot be lost or stolen. If you use a palm, Blackberry, or PDA, keep it on *masked* or *hidden*, where you'll have to use a password to reveal it. There are great, new encryption programs which can safely protect passwords, credit card numbers, phone numbers, and more from prying eyes. Same goes for your computer. There are certain items your boss will not want out of the house. If you use a laptop and keep information on it, make sure you have to log in a password before it can be accessed. Go over all of this with your employer and make sure you are both on the same page.

- **Emergency Info**

You'll need to have a list at your fingertips of emergency contacts. This includes doctors, children's doctors, hospital numbers, insurance and insurance card information, nearest hospital locations and numbers, allergies, medicines, and prescriptions, immediate family members. This list may also include fire and police in your neighborhood. It could also include locksmith, plumber, glass repair, auto towing, etc.

▪ Contacts

Keep a contact list which includes business associates, family members, friends, restaurants, spas, hotels, contractors, schools, again, doctors, pharmacies, florists, etc. See Chapter 17 under *Laminated Lists of Important Contacts.*

▪ A, B, C, Lists of Important People

What is the idea behind the ABC List? It's merely a way for you to know when to bother your boss with a matter or call. His business may depend on having immediate access to certain people in his field and vice-versa. In his personal world, he may have some friends who are closer, and more important to him than others. The same may go for his family. He may have one brother he's closer to than the other. Part of your duty as the gatekeeper is insulating your boss. Again, this never needs to be handled in a curt or rude manner. In fact, you need to make sure that while you're screening your employer from people, at the same time you are making each and every one of them feel like they're the most important person to your boss. Why? Because you are the face of your boss. You are representing his interests.

The list goes as follows: A people are announced. B people may sometimes be announced and sometimes you will tell them he or she is in a meeting or tied up. "She wishes she could talk, is there a number she can call you back at?" B people might be a relative, someone important they met with last week at an event. Put them on hold and check with your boss. Very quickly you'll get a sense of how to handle them. C people get a message taken. C People might be contractors, sales people, a doctor's appointment.

Follow-Up And Follow-Thru

At 2am, when you are finally getting some well deserved rest, you are brought out of your much needed sleep by the annoying sound of the phone. Your boss is wondering why she doesn't have the reservations you were to arrange. She's in Las Vegas with some important friends and the club they are going to does not have them on the list. What do you do?

Always, always, always, Follow up and follow through. It's not only about making sure all the aspects of the trip are handled, but making sure that all reservations are confirmed, that everyone involved is on the same page and has all the information; your boss, the club, the limo driver. Get names, re-confirm, write it down, include the last date and time you spoke with someone. Remember, if it can fall through the cracks, it will.

Make Your Job Easier

Resources are a vital part of your job. Know how to get something fast. Keep a growing file of contacts who know specific things; plumbers, handyman, auto shop, travel agent, specialty tailor, etc. Make sure you keep good relationships with vendors and contractors so that when you need something fast, they will come to your aid.

You're Expected To Know Everything

Is it unreasonable to ask something of you and expect you to know the answer? Of course. But knowing that you will be given some challenging tasks, the real question is; can you figure out how to get it done?

A lot will be asked and expected of you. A great deal of which you may not know how to do or don't know where to begin. To be successful you are going to have to be resourceful and learn how and where to get the answers. A big part of your position will be delegating to others who do know how to handle a specific task. You are not always expected to do everything yourself but you are expected to get it done. Your network will help your gather the resources to accomplish this, but in the beginning you may also need to do research and build a resourceful team of your own.

Being resourceful is also a matter of figuring out how to find the answer, where to look for the source. Example: If you're asked; "What's the name of that Sushi place with the funny hostess on Westwood Blvd?"

Where do you start? You could begin by SMS Googling "Sushi" and "Westwood Blvd." Next you might try "Japanese" and "Westwood Blvd." Next try going to Google on the Internet. Can you add any information? "Japanese restaurant on Westwood blvd. near the crest theater" Since you know it's near the Crest Theater can you call them and ask the name of the restaurant? Do you have time to drive by there and look? Is there a friend of your boss's you can ask that has eaten there?

There are many ways to begin searching for your query but whatever the results you need to at least try. And the better Personal Assistant will use many creative resources to get the answers.

So what's the point of going to so much trouble for such a minor task? Well it's your job of course but more to the point if you really think about it, you are also honing some skills which can not only make you very useful, but a valuable commodity. Who knows where you'll end up next, and when competition is involved it's good to have the edge. (Not a Sun Tzu quote)

Chapter 7:
Your Position

What Kind Of Personal Assistant Are You Becoming?

Are you a leader or a follower? Working for someone in a powerful position means that you too need to be a powerful person. You must have the ability to take charge of every situation; you need to be able to put a team together. You need to delegate.

Think of this as a company. The household or estate you work at is the company, your employer is the CEO and to be successful he needs the best team (staff) to run his company. He needs leaders who can take charge of the workers and see that the widgets are being manufactured in a timely, cost efficient way that will only improve his bottom line.

In hiring you he or she is intrusting you with leading and managing a team, whether it's the household staff, the day laborers, outside contractors, or being part of the team that is overseeing a project, whether that's a dinner party, or building a guest house. You are a point person for your employer and he is counting on you to represent him as a leader of his organization.

How Assertive Should You Be?

In addressing assertiveness one must also look at diplomacy. Of course it always depends who it is you are dealing with. A boss will want a team member who is strong, confident, and efficient like them. Sometimes he will want you to stand up for your beliefs and convictions and sometimes you will need to know when to step back and let the situation work itself out.

There will be moments when you need to get it done absolutely, positively, with no exceptions. And there will be times when that is just not possible.

Keep in mind assertive never means being rude, being a bully, belittling someone, or just plain being mean. But assertive also doesn't mean letting someone roll right over you or take advantage of you.

Example: In some cities like New York there are times when store employees just don't care about service. You go to Williams Sonoma asking for White dish towels only to be told they don't have any by some annoying kid who doesn't care. Never take no as the final answer. Always ask someone else. You'll be surprised at how many times you end up finding what you want. If you don't see a specific video on the store shelf, poke around before giving up and look behind other videos, look on the end racks, maybe someone even put one down in the wrong place. Be creative, but be vigilant.

Chapter 8:
Becoming Indispensable

Little Things That Make You Shine

It can be as simple as washing a dirty glass in the sink and putting it away, or, filling the car with gas. Little can also mean putting the latest updated schedule on your boss's desk so it's the first thing he sees when he arrives. Maybe it's having his favorite beverage stocked in the fridge. These small details can seem trite, and sometimes you may not hear anything about it, but your boss will appreciate your attention to detail. Keep in mind that a big part of your job is keeping your boss as stress free as possible, and one of the best ways to do this is to anticipate something before he comes to you and asks you to go out and get it.

Are You Clairvoyant?

After a while, you'll begin to read what kind of mood your boss is in and often you will know why. So mind reading is simply the technique of anticipating this before it comes up. For example, if the weather is becoming colder, start preparing their sweaters and jackets, and begin preparing to put away summer items. If you know that after a stressful day your boss likes to unwind by plopping down into their favorite chaise lounge with a bowl of Hagan Daaz and a good video. So, have the ice cream and video ready to go. If he regularly eats out n Friday nights, have a couple reservations at his favorite places secured. You can always cancel.

Be Prepared!

Always have a spare pen or pencil with you. Always have a little cash for parking or change for the meter. If you drive your boss, keep extra water, gum, Chap Stick, aspirin, and sometimes an additional cell phone or battery handy for her.

Try to envision what your day will be like. Actually picture yourself going through the motions. This can help you plan better for what's to come. For example, if you know that tomorrow you are going to be driving your boss from Malibu to Downtown Los Angeles, does the car have a working spare tire? Is there washer fluid for the windows? Gas in the car? Do you have a map with you? Have you checked the day's traffic conditions? Maybe at the last minute your boss wants you to come with him. Do you have a sport coat ready to go in case you meet with clients?

Envisioning the day can help you plan and prepare for many of these events.

Knowing When To Be Invisible

There is a golden rule, *"Do not speak unless spoken to."* As a Personal Assistant this may not be the case for you, but you may need to practice, *"Remain in the background until needed."* Some positions will require you to be in sight at all times. Others will want you to stay out of sight until needed. Sometimes it is because they want to feel like their home is still theirs. Sometimes your employers just need some down or alone time. Learn to be sensitive to your employers needs and try to work on accommodating their desires even if sometimes it's unspoken.

Secrets Of The Trade

Scotty from the original Star Trek always comes to mind. Whenever the captain ask for something Scotty would always claim that it is nearly impossible to do and it will take weeks. When the captain says they only have hours and Scotty does pull through, he looks like a god.

It is good to always have things in your arsenal for such occasions. For example, let's say you are traveling with your boss and you are out and about in another State or country. There are no power cords around, no chargers, etc. and of course, his cell phone dies. His battery ran out. He forgot his earbuds. But what if you kept an extra battery with you? How about keeping a second cell phone incase his breaks? A back-up hearing aid? A spare shirt? Of course you can't always carry everything with you, but you can have it nearby or plan out your trip by finding a local place that can get a replacement fast! Again, visualize. Picture the place you will be traveling to and try to think about what might be needed on the trip. Before you leave for your destination, research what stores are in the area that can be useful to you.

If you are on a film shoot in another city or country. Do you have access to the same water your boss drinks when at home? Do the hotels have the same pillows your boss is used to and will have to sleep on for six to eight months? Can you find his favorite shoes if his get wreaked? Think about, foods, movies, medicines, software, batteries, etc.

A good Personal Assistant will have this all on hand or know how to get it. A great Personal Assistant can do it faster. Looking like a star is all in the preparation. Don't rely on others to have the things you may need. Take it upon yourself to have all of this ready or know how to get it before the trip.

> **SECRET:** Want to know one of the best tools you can have with you at all times? Something that will always come in handy and save you again and again? And, it only costs $2.00? This valuable tool will be used more than anything else you can pull out of your bag of tricks. So what is it? A small pocket-sized notebook and pencil. You'll be surprised at how many times this handy yet simple item will become the most useful of tools. Have you ever had a boss call you and start riffling off a million ideas and things they need? Or you might be running around and someone calls and you need to take down a message or their phone number. Sure, you can do this with a PDA but try typing on those tiny keypads while driving or while your boss is talking at light speed.

You will have many other things to deal with as well, travel arrangements, contacts, documents, scheduling, clothing, and more, but this is just one more tool that can alleviate some of the strain when these obstacles come at you fast.

Chapter 9:
Travel

You may go or you may need to stay at the home or office and tend to things while your employer is away. Whatever you do, you will still need to have a handle on all aspects of the travel and be well prepared to deal with any changes or last minute surprises.

How To Prepare

Once you know who will be traveling, when, where, and for how long, you can begin to build your list of details and build a schedule and travel itinerary that you can handle from the road, the office, or the home.

You will need to know if he desires to pay with credit cards or use miles. Do you know how to transfer miles? How to upgrade them? How to check them in at the airport, fast? Do you know what an airport escort is?

Flyer Miles: A number of people who travel frequently will have flying points often referred to as frequent flyer miles. Each airline has a different name for them but essentially the passenger has points on their airline account they can redeem to fly instead of paying with currency. Points or miles can sometimes be used to upgrade the passenger from economy to business, business to first class. You'll need to learn how this works by calling or going onto the airlines web site and researching their rules and regulations.

Some airlines will allow you to swap miles with other airline partners, some will let you trade using credit card services such as American Express (though they have specific airlines they work with). You can also get creative and look at services such as *Points.com* a program that allows you to trade mileage points with non-affiliated airlines.

Airport Escort: This is someone who will meet your employer and his party at the airline and help to make their transition to the plane or airline lounge, smooth, easy, and hassle free. An Airport Escort will handle all of your luggage and expedite you through security. They stay with you every step of the way until you are safely and comfortably on your plane. They will check if there are any upgrades available (sometimes at no extra charge), and when it's time to board, they will notify you and escort you to the boarding gate.

Hotel preferences: Does your boss like to stay on a higher floor? Or have his room away from the elevators? Does he need a fax machine, favorite water? Does he want a view? Are his favorite pillows in the room? Is the room hypoallergenic? Where does the sun rise or set? Is he near the pool? Away from the ice machine? Down the hall from the elevator? Find out!

Auto rental: Does he prefer a new car or an older one? Do you know which rental agencies carry which brands of vehicles? Do they have towing service? Navigation system? Can anyone drive the vehicle?

You may also be responsible for packing, making an itinerary list, preparing snacks for the trip, and having some useful items available for your boss to take with him; eye mask, ear plugs, power cords, tissues, aspirin, etc.

Carefully go over everything. There are so many times someone has packed a suit, tie, shirts, socks, and shoes, but forgot something as simple as a belt. Also, when packing toiletries, pay attention to sizes. Know if your boss is taking a carry on that she will need to have the smaller toothpaste and shampoo. Check with the airlines before packing and get the latest information on rules and regulations. However, traveling private is different and other regulations apply.

Who To Prepare

It is your job to know all of your boss's travel habits. How he likes to fly, what his favorite airlines are, what color seats he prefers (yes, I said it). Aisle or window preference, what foods he can eat, where he likes to sit (First Class or Business), time of day he prefers to travel.

Not only will you need to prepare the people going on the trip, but you may need to alert business associates, staff, and others that your boss will be traveling. If there is a staff, this is also the time to keep an extra vigil on them and keep the house running smoothly and making sure they don't take this as a mini-vacation. While it is okay to let them ease up a bit, it is important that the house continues to run efficiently.

If there is a second home, alert that staff and make sure everything will be ready when your employer arrives; food, clean sheets, fuel in the cars, etc.

Also, contact the limo service that will be meeting your boss. Get the name and number of the driver's cell. Make sure he is on time and give him a description of what your employer is wearing so he can easily find him. Ask the driver to have a sign with your employer's name.

Discuss with your employer anything she may want you to deal with while she's away.

Last Minute Change Of Plans

If you are not using a travel agent, and even if you are, you will need to keep a specific itinerary of everything that is occurring on the trip so you can accommodate any changes or surprises that arise. The airport may be snowed in. There may be an overbooking at the hotel, someone in the traveling party may get sick, an unscheduled business appointment, death in the family, or household disaster may arise, and you will need to change plans fast.

Occasionally you may have one of those very very rare boss's who only flies on planes with red seat cushions and he has just boarded a plane with blue ones. Or the flight is delayed and he wants another one fast. Keeping a good itinerary with as many details as you can have will help make last minute switching a lot easier. Still challenging, but easier.

Do You Go Or Stay?

One of the things you should work out before hand is knowing if you will be traveling with your boss. Some of you may want to travel, and some may not. You may have a family and want to be home every night. These are important things you'll need to discuss when first taking the position.

Working Mobile

On the go should never mean out of touch. You need to be able to have as much ability as you can to stay in touch on every front, phone contact, email, fax, messaging, weather, travel info, etc.

Fortunately, we are in a very technologically savvy world and it is easy to do so. The question is, are you technically savvy? Can you figure out how to get email while nowhere near a computer? Can you find out the weather from inside a taxi?

Again, you will need to discuss with your employer everything that will be expected of you in this area and then make sure they can supply you with or have you purchase the items necessary to help keep him or her in the know. And, if you don't know the best items to purchase, then your job is to find the tech savvy person who can tell you what to get. A good source of information are web blogs or opinion web sites that can also rate these products.

Secondly, you need to make sure these new tech items can work in the places you will be traveling to. It will do you no good to have a Blackberry that works in New York and not in Spain, or North Carolina. You need to make sure that you have an idea of not only where the items may be used, but in what capacity.

Living Out Of A Bag

You are responsible for yourself, your boss, and possibly his family, associates, band members, etc. So while you want to travel light, you need to make sure you bring things that you will need when away for a while. If you are staying in hotels, most concierge can get you items you may need. But don't buy too much because you may need to leave early and you have to be able to pack up and get out quickly. Think of it like an episode of the Apprentice.

You may need to pack every day, so learn to take only those items really necessary and figure out how to get the rest later.

I Want The Food I Get Back Home!

There are just going to be times when both you and your boss will want exactly what you get back home. Sometimes this is easy to handle, sometimes you will need to work a little harder to get these items, which can also entail higher costs, and then sometimes you still can't find the item.

See if there is something you could use to substitute. Perhaps you can't get whey protein but you can get egg protein. Maybe there is no agave sweetener, and your boss might be okay using dates to sweeten their protein shake for the time being. If your employer uses a chef or dietician, you can call or email them and get some ideas for good alternatives.

An actress was on location and just had to have a health shake that her trainer recommended. The problem was that some of the ingredients could not be found in that country and there was no way to rush ship the items needed. So, working through the night, her Personal Assistant, with input from the trainer, got together with some of the crew and came up with a mixture of other ingredients that ended up tasting like what they were missing. The actress never knew a thing.

Traveling With Children And Pets

A good travel agent can keep you up to date with the latest travel rules and regulations. When traveling with children, especially in today's security driven society, you should know a couple things. When traveling with a child and only one parent or no parents you will need to have a notarized letter from the parent(s) and you may need records from the physician saying it is okay to travel. If there are any medications, you should carry the proper documentation because they do baggage search nowadays for that as well.

Make sure you have any special reading materials, videos or other favorite items that will keep the child happy, and content as possible. Always have a sweater or light jacket with you and there are times when a quick change of clothes is with you on board the plane for any "accidents" that may occur. Also, children touch everything. Have them wash their hands often and make sure you do the same. Always carry wipes with you.

For pets you will also need all the proper documentation and every airline can tell you their specific requirements. I suggest you call twice. There have been a number of times when an assistant will be told one thing and something completely different when they arrive. So verify your information, get a name, id number and location where the office you spoke with is.

Checking the weather can be most important especially when traveling long distances. The temperatures inside the cargo area can change and you want to make sure the animal is always as comfortable as possible. If you are traveling private, the pet will travel within the cabin.

The good things is that some commercial airlines are getting on board and offering incentives for smaller pets to ride inside the cabin along with you. However this can all change if your pet is rowdy, noisy, or smells badly.

Home Sick

This is a tough area for anyone who will be on the road for months at a time. Sometimes it got so bad for me I would have my roommate video tape my dog and FedEx them to me wherever I was.

Find the time to keep up with friends and relatives. Fortunately, cell phones make it easier these days to do those long distance calls.

Another thing that can help with travel blues is to have people send you letters. There is something comforting about receiving a letter or even a silly care package with goofy things in it. Yes, it will make you sad but mostly fond of the people who took the time to make you feel wanted.

It is important that the position you take is one you like and not one you took because it's cool or because you're working for a big star. If you do not enjoy your job, you will really get homesick when you are away for long period of time.

Chapter 10:
Lord of the Manner

Lessons On Managing Houses, Estates, And Mansions

There may be an Estate Manager for the household. There may be a Major Domo, a Household Manager, or a Head Butler. As a Personal Assistant, you may be asked to work for or with any of these people. If none of these exist, depending on the size of the home, you as the Personal Assistant may be required to perform a number of the duties listed below. It's best to review and get familiar with what might be expected of you.

Household Managers took their place in American mansions and estates of the rich and famous modeled after "butlers" found in Europe. They ensure that the home runs smoothly. They may be the only staff in the house, which means they may clean, provide wardrobe and linen care, run errands, and/or cook; they may also schedule contractors, organize dinners and parties, and/or oversee finances. Or they may supervise other household staff.

If one of your duties as a Personal Assistant is to oversee the household you may provide supervisory and administrative responsibilities for the home and family. In a home with a larger staff, the House Manager will usually work in a more administrative position, but as the Personal Assistant, you should always be ready to help out in case of staff illness, vacation, or vacancy.

You need to possess a pleasant demeanor, strong work ethic, excellent organizational skills, and a confident attitude to succeed. When running a household you'll need to be completely flexible in meeting any and all needs of the family. It may be necessary to have a knowledge of different styles of formal entertaining (different styles), protocol, purchasing high-quality items for the family's use, vast resources to fit any occasion, etc. You very well may be responsible for managing more than one home and provide continuity between homes or properties.

You'll be in charge of directing correspondence to and from the employer; scheduling appointments with the employer, and any maintenance work to be done on the home; which can include tracking the family and household finances; making travel arrangements and developing itineraries; and any other personal request the employer may make.

You could be called upon to oversee the work of the staff, checking to make sure they are doing their work to the best of their abilities or deciding if the staff require further education. In order to supervise properly, you should have a good understanding of all the duties and responsibilities of any staff member.

Your duties can also include typing letters and memos, answering the phone and taking messages, opening, sorting and/or answering mail, setting up and managing files for letters and other important documents, scheduling appointments, or any other kind of clerical work. You may also act as bookkeeper and manage the family budget, track expenses, manage records for tax purposes, research and keep track of investments, or obtain quotes on major renovations of the home. In this case you'll need to have excellent computer capabilities and should maintain extensive warranty and inventory files, keep track of repairs, maintain a Household Bible (Household Management Reference Book).

Another task is personal shopping for the lady or gentleman of the house. They should be well aware that the shopping habits of the wealthy and powerful are far different from the average person's shopping habits. A wealthy family has no problem setting aside a half-million dollars, or more, in the budget for their personal needs. They may think nothing of seeking out an antique chest of drawers and paying $80,000.00+ for it, purchasing multiple sets of fine china or an extensive silver collection, spending $5000.00 on a single set of bed linens, remodeling any part of the home at a moment's notice, or spending $100,000.00 on a Halloween party or $1,500.00+ for fresh flowers for the week.

You may be asked to research and implement new security needs for the home. Not only plan the family vacation to Italy, but also go along. Or you may simply listen attentively and sympathetically—with open ears and a closed mouth—as your employer bemoans their difficulties of a particular day. You may arranging dinner reservations, having medication delivered, calling the insurance agent, or pick up the children.

Your job is to also respect the sanctity of your relationship with your employer and keep all conversations and experiences confidential—essential when working with the rich and famous. Do nothing to compromise it; above all, be trustworthy.

If you have a housekeeper, they are the backbones of the fabulous mansions and estates of the wealthy. A beautifully cared-for home is the work of one or more housekeeper. A housekeeper's tasks entail all the facets of serving a wealthy employer and keeping a home in such a way that it will not just be clean and neat, but will also shine in a way that only a well-cared for home can and be protected from damage. The housekeeper does anything necessary to maintain an impeccable appearance in a home and to ensure the value of the possessions trusted in their care.

No celebrity homeowner need worry that their fine home furnishings and valuable home accessories will be damaged with a professional housekeeper is working for them. They know how to care for fine linens, marble, crystal, silver, and other valuable materials.

Good food is essential to making any house a home, and this is especially true in the lifestyles of the rich and famous. The family Chef understands this most basic of all needs and is able to make it a reality. They are responsible for the meals and everything this entails: menu planning, proper selection of the freshest produce and meats, pantry shopping, kitchen clean-up and organization, and care and purchase of any necessary equipment and supplies.

The best Chef is one who can meet any of their wealthy employer's wants and needs. They are able to prepare food according to special dietary needs, anything from home-style to gourmet meals, or special occasions, formal dinners, and cocktail parties. They will be proficient in food presentation and be able to set an "inviting table." They should be flexible enough to work with kids or pets under their feet or to work in coordination with a caterer. Indeed, flexibility is key for a good Chef.

When a wealthy and powerful homeowner has several different properties, it becomes necessary for an Estate Manager to maintain continuity between all the households. This is entirely an administrative management position. This person will have expert knowledge of personnel and home management, property care, and grounds expertise.

The Estate Manager supervises many different properties that are fully staffed, possibly making final decisions in hiring and firing staff, and will undoubtedly be called upon to set the standards for service throughout the home(s).

They will usually be responsible for any renovations on the properties, hiring contractors, and researching and making recommendations for any major purchases, i.e., investment antiques, yachts, airplanes, polo ponies, the design of the expansive new water garden, stables, or the wiring of the entire house to make it a "Smart Home".

The Estate Manager can sometimes also be the wealthy employer's Personal Assistant, acting as the "right-hand person," which would entail the usual errands, money management, personal shopping, and anything else the employer desires.

The Estate Manager also known as the Major Domo is hired to manage all the affairs of one or more large estates. This person must have a very strong administrative and managerial background, be well versed in business and social etiquette, have strong communication skills and must have very good computer skills.

The responsibilities of an Estate Manager involve the direct day-to-day management of the household including the supervision, scheduling, hiring and firing of staff as well as making purchasing decisions for all household items from linens to furniture. The estate manager is responsible for overseeing all aspects of ongoing renovations or new construction being undertaken on any of the estates and has to work in collaboration with architects, designers, contractors and so on. She/he is required to plan all aspects of estate events ranging from social gatherings to birthday parties, and must make arrangements for catering, transportation and accommodations for the guests attending these events. She/he may also be called upon to research and make recommendations on some important undertakings that the employer may be considering which may involve anything from buying a yacht to building a new home theater. Other responsibilities involve overseeing the care and preservation of the fine art and antiques on each estate, the supervision of estate accounts and expenses as well as maintaining all paperwork for payroll, petty cash and all records to be submitted to the accountants.

As a Personal Assistant you may be called upon to perform a number of duties that are similar to that of the Estate Manager.

Information provided here is credited to the *Professional Domestic Services & Institute*

Overseeing The Staff

If one of your responsibilities is to oversee the staff, then you need to have several skills under your belt. As a leader you will need to be able to delegate, you'll have to be organized, tactful, and you will need to be someone that people want to follow.

Anyone can boss people around but you need to see that the job is done right, completed on time, and most importantly to your employer's satisfaction. Also, don't just assign a task and then remove yourself until it's completed. You will be responsible for checking the progress of the job and making sure there are no mistakes or miscommunications along the way. In the end, as the point person, it all comes back to you.

Dealing With Contractors

Contractors can make or break you as well. When they come into the home environment you are inviting a stranger to your boss's private space. You need to screen and monitor these people carefully, especially if they are new. Never leave a new contractor alone. Always have someone watching and overseeing them. This may not always be possible but it is always important to remember.

Again, treat these people with courtesy and respect. Offer them water when they arrive. Make sure they understand what is needed of them.

They are there to do a job for your boss and you are the face they will see the most. You need to keep the environment protected at all times. Any items they bring into the home that could potentially scratch floors, knock something over, chip or tear furniture, or bring dust or debris into the house, you are ultimately responsible for and must prepare for any and all of these.

It doesn't matter how big or important you think you or your employer are, he could be the biggest box office star, if the contractor messes up because they do not like you, it is still you that has to answer for it. So treat them graciously but the reins are still in your hands.

Treat Their Home Like Your Own

Assuming you're not a slob, the point here is to respect the home you're working in. Saying "Treat it like your own home" does not mean kicking your feet up and watching a movie on the big screen. It means that you wouldn't let anyone disrespect the place you live and when you are in charge of someone else's space, the same goes. While you will eventually know intimate details of your employer's life and have access to their world, you still need to treat their home and office with respect and courtesy.

Letitia Baldrige, the foremost expert on manners and decorum, says to show respect to the person trusting you in their home. That means be courteous to the staff, don't snoop, do not hop up on the counter, lean your chair back, help yourself to food or drink. Unless or until you and your employer establish how to act in their home, you need to show that you are respectful of them and their family.

It also lets them know how you will behave when they send you to act as their representative when meeting business associates, delivering gifts to friends, or dropping their children off at a friend or neighbors. You, are a direct reflection of your employer and respecting their home is the first step to showing that.

Chapter 11:
A Sample "Day in the Life..."

As I've mentioned before there is no typical day, but every day is unique and unusual. Yes, there are repetitive, mundane days when you will be envious of your friends who played hooky to run off to Vegas for the weekend.

Since every day is so unique and different I'm going to share two completely different days with you and hope that you will not only enjoy the stories (all true), but glean a little something to take with you.

A former boss was traveling for two weeks. Travel time is usually the perfect time to get projects done on the house while they're away; construction, additions, modifications, repairs, painting, and more. My tasks were to have new carpet padding put in the entire house, Have several new light fixtures hung, get a professional out to set up the new home theater system, and my employer also says for me to take some time for myself to unwind. Yeah, right.

So, first things first, since the house was already furnished I, being a resourceful Personal Assistant, needed to hire a crew to come in and help me to move all the furniture out so the carpeting could be pulled up and the new padding put down. Additionally, the was a strange conduit in the middle of the floor in what was going to be the entertainment room where the home theater was going and the conduit needed to be removed. So I started with that.

The electrician came and I told him what we needed and he began his work. The house was older and when he got rid of the wires and conduit, it wasn't until afterwards that we found that almost half the wiring in the house was tied to this. So now I was stuck with no power for almost half of the outlets in the entire house. And now begins the newest project. Rerunning new wiring to complete the power. During this time we also learned that a number of these outlets also weren't grounded and didn't have up to code wiring. A bigger project indeed.

The next wrench in the works was that the crew I hired to move the furniture didn't show. Couldn't reach them, couldn't track them down. So I immediately called some friends who said they could round up some guys fast because I figured if they came very early the next morning before the carpet crew we could get it done. Late that same night, I get a call that they all get called to work on a new show and need to be on set first thing in the morning. No one would be showing up.

I spent that night moving most of the stuff myself. About eighty percent of it. I decided that when the carpet crew came I would throw money at them to help move some of the heavier items. It worked and they helped, but it made their workday longer and slowed things down for me. Additionally, the electrician's bill was slowly rising as this became a harder and harder project for him, and also slower as he couldn't go into a room until the carpet crew was finished in there.

Eventually everything turned out good but it put me way behind, I never got my down time, and I spent more money than we had anticipated. So while my boss very was happy with the results, he wasn't happy about the extra money spent. Even though it wasn't my fault, I was certainly tied into the emotion of the event. After that the home theater turned out great and that made him feel better about the whole event.

On the flip side, I did something that was so simple for me to handle that the reward seemed insane. At the time I was working for Jewel's mother who was also her manager at the time, and they were going to see some friends for a night of dinner and a movie. Because of our location, an island, the only way to get to the restaurant and movie was via a puddle jumper, a small plan that takes them to another island and from there a limo would pick them up and take them to their destination.

So all I had to do is book the restaurant, I made a special call to reserve seats in the theater - which can sometimes be done with a little finessing. I also had to take care of scheduling the plane and transportation to and from the pickup and landing areas. Everything went great. I even workout it out up front with the restaurant so they would not have to pay and I would take care of the meal.

They were so happy that the next day they gave me the day off and offered to fly me to the same theatre to see the movie, which at the time I think was Spiderman. I got to bring a date, so basically for me and a date to see Spiderman the movie; it costs roughly $300 for the day. It was a fun perk and what a fun story it was to tell everyone I actually took a plane and town car to the movies!

Okay, Let's Try That Again

Everyone, in every job, at some point will have a bad day or bad experience. A day or even a week when things just won't go right. People may yell, it all may rain down on you. The first instinct is to stop at the nearest bar or run home close the drapes, get out the TiVo remote and binge eat. Instead, take an evening to decompress. Relax, chill, and try to put the day out of your mind. In-other-words, regroup. When things look less daunting, re-examine everything that happened and still, don't act on it just yet. Review what transpired or even better, write it down. Once you can objectively look at what went wrong, you can figure out if there was something different you could do the next time or if there was just no way to stop things from spiraling down.

Whatever the case, the results are the same; your employer may be mad and upset with you but you can go on and know better how to handle things the next time around. You aren't going to be able to fix or solve everything, and there are times it is simply someone else's issue. If you take everything to heart, and make it personal you will not enjoy your time as a Personal Assistant and eventually you will either become depressed or keep leaving positions hoping to find the right, nurturing job.

Instead, learn from the incident, try to grow a thicker skin, and realize that things will arise that are out of your control. But what you can do is re-examine the situation and prepare for the next time.

So When's The Next 12 Step Meeting?

This is a job where very often you are going to feel alone. Because of the confidentiality agreement you signed, you can't really go and pour out your soul to your friends. Yet you need an outlet where you don't feel so isolated and that no one gets or understands what you're going through.

Networking can be an important tool for keeping you on a good track. Again, while you can't really divulge everything that takes place for you day to day, you can ask advice, get opinions, or feedback on how to handle something.

It also doesn't hurt to meet with peers in the field who can go for a drink or dinner and just talk and commiserate. You position has so many aspects to it, so many responsibilities, that you will and can get overwhelmed. The trick is not to feel alone or isolated. You also need to pay attention and acknowledge the successes of the job and all the things you've done that give you and your position value. Take pride, this is a hard job to do and harder than most because you are often on your own. Very few other jobs has a person doing so many different things at once, in such creative, innovative ways.

Chapter 12:
The Perks

About Those Holidays...

Everyone is different. Some Personal Assistants get most holidays off. Some work almost every holiday. Either traveling, or if in town, the Personal Assistant can be responsible for the shopping, gift buying, groceries or catering, making sure the house is decorated or set up, gifts delivered during the holidays, helping the nanny with the children, or being in charge of the staff who are also working.

This is another area that is best discussed up front when you are first negotiating the roles of your position.

If this is a chance for you to miss a dreaded family gathering, then great. But if you're close to your family, your spouse, fiancée, or pet, and don't want to miss the holidays, you'd better speak up now, because if they can use you, they will.

Rewards of The Job

Everyone has a different idea of rewards. For some it is staying in luxury hotels when traveling. For others, their reward can be in flying only on private jets with their employer. Some look forward to the paid holidays. There are Personal Assistants who work out monetary compensation, or a per diem, when they travel and there are a few who saved this money to buy new cars or put down payments on houses. A few like the perk of being invited to a premier or an exclusive party. Some are given the very stylish hand-me-downs that their boss no longer wants or needs; clothing, jewelry, shoes. Others are sometimes given the "White Elephant" gifts their boss didn't care for; brand new DVD players, stereos, Manolo Blahniks, complete kitchen sets, or certificates to spas, hotels, or restaurants. There are any number of rewards on this job. But you shouldn't ever expect these.

Gifts

There will be times when you've just busted your hump, working hard all year, going the extra mile, working overtime with little pay or accolades, and come holiday time, you see a big whooping $100, and think; "You've got to be kidding me."

There will also be times when your boss is generous for generous sake, gifting you a brand new Cartier, and there will be times when you get the hand-me-downs which can really be great. Items he or she may not want or need, great clothing, watches, a nice dinner, a great party.

A gift should never be expected but always appreciated. You might get the lamest of paperweights or the SAG awards gift bag, but whatever it is, your performance shouldn't be affected by whether you receive something or not. That being said, if you've been at a position for a while and *no* appreciation is being shown to you, I don't mean being there just a month or so, but if you've been with an employer for a while who can show no thanks or appreciation, you may want to reevaluate if you should stay or move along. Eventually the glamour of any job will wear off and you will see it without rose colored glasses. The point is that while the life of a Personal Assistant can be exciting, it is still a job and there will be times when you will feel it.

Connections

One of the most valuable things you'll get from your job are the contacts and connections established throughout your time at any given position. Some Personal Assistants may often go into another field of endeavor such as writing, producing, consulting, directing, and they now have some valuable, amazing resources to help them get a leg up.

Chapter 13:
Ready To Move Up?

I'm Just Using This As A Stepping-Stone

If you are someone who's using your situation to get a foot in the door or you've found that you now have an interest in being a producer as you've had the opportunity to see how they work, you need to do this tactfully and make sure that until you leave, your boss is still your primary objective. You should also remember that while she may hate losing you, she's often in a prime position to help you with your new career endeavors.

Whether you are making a career as a Personal Assistant or just using it to move forward, this is a great place to meet many people in a variety of fields and to learn a large number of new skill sets. In a year, if you are smart, you'll be much farther along in what you know and who you know. And, if you play your cards right, your boss can help you achieve your new dreams and desires.

There are times when you and your boss cannot go any farther with your position. There is just no room for growth. It is this time that the two of you need to discuss this and reevaluate your position. Perhaps you want to further yourself but there is no upward job or enough finances to take you to the next level. If you are doing a good job and have been together a while it should be okay to sit down with your employer and discuss the direction you are going.

Chapter 14:
How To Never Get Fired

I wish this was the one time that there was a magic bullet. But alas, there is no sure-proof way to keep from being fired. What you can do, however, is to make yourself valuable. By keeping the home and office running smoothly, maintaining well-organized records, files, and logs, by taking pride in the appearance of the home or office, and by making sure everyone from staff to business associates are treated with respect and cared for, you will give your employer a sense of pride in having you on her team. You'll be giving her a reason to recognize how well managed her life is and see that you really care about being a team player. While ultimately, this is no guarantee for securing any job, barring any unforeseen circumstances, it's the best way to assure longevity in your position. Take pride in what you do and continue to be a team player. You'll go far and become someone who is highly sought after.

No Job Is Secure

That being said, no job is secure. For whatever reason, no matter how irrational, no matter how unfair, stupid, or selfish you can lose your job at any time. It happens. Inflation, deflation, your boss himself was fired, a bad divorce, a break-up, death in the family, whatever, there will be times when you are powerless and you may lose your position.

So how can you safeguard yourself? Work on building a career and resume that shows you are valuable. Do your best and keep doing it. While length of time is a vital aspect when someone is looking to hire you, it is not the only thing and they will take everything into account. So don't anticipate losing a job, just keep at it and make sure you are at your peak. In the meantime, save money to cushion yourself for the lean times.

Knowing When Your Time Is Winding Down

This job will take its toll. It will take a lot out of you. It will also give you so much in return. There are two types of Personal Assistants; those that stay with their employer for many years, George Clooney's assistant, Nicholas Cage's assistant, Rod Stewart's assistant, Billy Bob Thornton's assistant, Olympia Dukakis' assistant, and numerous others, all have been long-term Personal Assistants who still love what they do.

There are Personal Assistants who, on average, last anywhere from three to six years at a position. So what are the indicators that your time is running down? Every person is different, but if you notice that you are coming home every night and vegging for hours in front of the television, you aren't socializing as much as you used to, you are less passionate about things, friends can barely drag you out of the house anymore, then maybe it's time to reassess your situation. But also keep in mind that if you are someone who is a very empathic person, meaning someone who takes everything to heart, then you can find outlets to release those deep-rooted feelings. Learn to play more during your down time. Even when you're tired, find the time to go out and be with people you love. We've all had those times when we didn't want to go out but when we did, had a great time.

You need to find passions outside of your job. Are there any interests or hobbies you've been wanting to get involved in? Can you take a couple days of alone time to detox and get refreshed and reinvigorated? It's important that you find some personal time no matter how busy you are. Even if it means taking an hour in your day to call your family and touch base again. Go to a local coffee shop or tea emporium and chill, inhale the steam from your cup of tea, sip slowly, breathe, take it your surroundings, try to smile, relax your shoulders, lean back into your chair, and be in the moment.

No job is perfect, but you can take a step back and really examine why it feels like it's not working for you anymore. It may even take you speaking with your employer or his business manager, and in a calm and relaxed way let them know what's going on. You may laugh at this saying that your boss isn't the kind of person you can have a "chat" with. And that may be true, but do try to step outside of your situation and really examine what's going on. And if you say that you cannot take the time to step back, that in itself may be an indicator that your time *is* winding down, but if you can't learn to step outside the circle and look at what's going on objectively, you will likely take those same feeling and problems with you wherever you go.

Looking For A New Job (While Still At The Present One)

There's an old adage that the best time to look for work is when you're at... work. If you've decided you need to move on then you should use some time, while you still have an income, to begin searching for other opportunities. You also should have already started putting some savings aside in case it does take more time than you expected to find a new position.

You can discreetly hint around to contacts you've established throughout your career that you are looking to make a move. However, you DO NOT ever want to put your employer down or say anything negative about him

to anyone, especially while you're looking for a new job.
Why? Two reasons. First, you never know when
something will get back to him, and he'll hear of how
disgruntled you are (Reminder: You may need a referral
from him). Two, if you are talking smack about one boss,
your potential next employer may think you'll talk the
same about them one day.

As noted at in the beginning of this guide, you have some
tools to begin your job seeking research on line and
through networking. Again, Craig's List, Google, Monster,
placement agencies, headhunters, friends, relatives, the
waitress at your favorite coffee shop, your auto mechanic,
all can be good resources for your job hunt. You never
know who or where the next lead will come from.

Also, Never burn a bridge. What this means is that if you
decide to leave you should walk away from your position
with everything wrapped up nicely, all files completed, all
records neat and organized, all staff feeling protected and
respected. And your soon-to-be former employer needs to
feel like he is protected and not feel harmed by you. A
good Personal Assistant can rely on keeping good
relations with past employers and sometimes it benefits
them in their careers whether it's continuing as a Personal
Assistant or moving into a different occupation. There
have even been occasions where a Personal Assistant
returned to a prior position. Again, remember you may
also need a reference letter. So keep things light and
comfortable. Treat people with the same respect you
yourself would want in return.

Part 4:
Keep Your Value

Chapter 15:
Knowing Who's Who

You won't be expected to know everyone immediately, but you should start to create lists of who is important to your employer. Everyone is different. For some people, relatives come first. For others, they come last. You'll begin to get a sense of who is important to your boss by his reaction when you let him know who's trying to reach him.

Beyond that, depending what field your involved in, it also can benefit you and your employer by knowing; who the competition is, who his peers and associates are, whom he might be working with on an upcoming project. Read the news and periodicals that are relevant to your employers field.

Learning Your Boss's Habits

It's important to know your employer's habits, likes and dislikes. Remember earlier on when we talked about anticipating needs? The more you can get in tune with how he operates both in his business and personal world the better you will be at knowing when a mood is changing, or when you need to be sensitive to his needs.

Reading His Moods

Have you ever walked into a room and you could feel a mood shift and you thought "whoa…"? Or you meet someone for lunch and they are unusually quiet? Understanding someone's moods and how to properly respond can be a useful tool to have in your arsenal. It's not hard to do. You have been in a situation before where you knew something was off. Learn to gage the atmosphere when you come into the home or environment and pay attention to what is happening around you. If your employer is an athlete or actor, you may be able to read a mood by knowing how their game or performance went the day before. It could be that there was a family argument.

You won't be responsible for fixing a situation, but it's helpful to recognize when something is up, and when to lay low, hang back, or be quiet. Remember, you will often be closer to your boss in proximity and empathy than sometimes even a spouse can be. Be attuned to their surroundings and what is going on. They will appreciate you respecting their space.

Dealing with Allergies

Keeping a list of allergies and medicines can be important especially if your boss is someone always on the go. He or she might meet a large number of people every day, travel frequently, or have to attend many meetings where food is involved. If you have a list, you can prepare them for their day and also send them off with the proper antidote should they have a reaction to something. Climate and season can also be a factor.

This is also important if there are children in the picture. It's especially important to know what to do if the child has a reaction to something or has asthma. Keep a list of important people to call should a child have an allergic reaction.

Keeping Track Of Medications

One great way to be a top Personal Assistant is to keep records of medications and expiration dates. Have the prescribing doctor's and pharmacist' numbers handy too. If you and your employer travel, know the pharmacies that are close to where you are staying and make sure they carry your preferred brand. Some employers do not want the generic substitute. If you are ambitious, you can also check to see how much of a particular medication is left at the home. That will help you to determine when they will require a refill.

Their Favorite Things

Try to keep a growing list of favorites. Does he likes a certain restaurant? Does he also have a favorite waitress, maître d, desert, booth, wine, etc? Keep a list. Does he or she like to come home to fresh flowers? A late night snack? The lighting in the bedroom set just right?

Keeping A List Of:

- Food (Likes and Dislikes)
- Reoccurring Dates (The Oscars, Super Bowl, Black Friday)
- Birthdays
- Anniversaries
- Holidays
- Friends Annual Events
- Industry Happenings

This list above is pretty self explanatory. By keeping a visible list by your desk or in your daily planner, or on your computer, where you can see it on a regular basis, you can prepare for and give your employer a heads up of upcoming events. It will make your job easier too instead of rushing out at the last minute to by a birthday gift, or flowers, or having a clean suit or dress for an upcoming event.

Your job will rely heavily on lists, charts, calendars, and reminders. The more things you can place on a reminder list, the less you will have to do to plan and prepare for it. In fact, with a good lead time for reminding yourself that an event is pending, the easier it will be to take action on it. Texting your boss twelve days out a reminder that his brother's birthday is coming up gives him enough time to think of a gift. And, you enough time to buy, wrap, and send or deliver it.

Equipment

Make a file of all equipment purchased and create a sheet on how to use each item. Keep a file for all things purchased but more importantly keep the date, location, and any warranty information handy on the purchase. You need to have access to these things quickly.

Computers, Phones, PDAs, Etc.

Eventually all electronics will at some point have a hiccup. The best way to prepare for any incidentals is to:

a). Keep a list of all electronic equipment purchased; computers, phones, cell phones, fax machines, printers, TVs, DVD players, etc.
b). Keep a record of the purchase date, place of purchase, time, sales receipt & copy, serial numbers, any warranties or service agreement.
c). Maintain a list of phone numbers for warranties & service agreements, manufacturer's number, place of purchase, any and all tech support numbers. If you can, keep the original boxes the items came in.

d). Have a number for your own technician who you trust that can give you an accurate assessment of the issue.

Chapter 16: Resources To Hone Your Craft

Courses You Can Take

There are not many classes out there on being a Personal Assistant, in fact, less than a handful, but this is not the only area where you will need an education. However, check out:

Kerri Campos Consulting: www.kerricampos.com

PDSI: www.housestaff.net

CPAI: www.celebritypersonalassistants.com

Starkey International Institute: www.starkeyintl.com

Lifestyle Resources: www.sterlinglifestyle.com

Depending on the position and the duties that will be required of you, you may need to take other courses which can only strengthen your position; travel, computers, gift wrapping, electronics courses, security, etc. And if it is directly relevant to the position you are in, you should discuss with your employer about his picking up the tab.

Also, depending on your roll, there is value to taking household management courses, domestic courses, courses on private and commercial travel, working with contractors, computer and technology courses and more. It would also be good to have some emergency medical classes as well. CPR, if there are children and they swim, life guard courses. Some general first aid can also be useful.

Again, anything that would be relevant to your position and make you a valued asset to your employers will be invaluable. You can find many courses on what you need in your local area; First Aid – Red Cross, Swimming – YMCA, Travel – A reputable Travel Agency, Electronics – The Geek Squad (or similar organization), Computers – Apple Store (or similar organization).

Books You Can Use

The good thing about today's society is that there is a book on almost everything. There are many on running and maintaining a household. How to shop, how to dress, there are books on auto repair, and while you shouldn't do the work yourself, it is good to have a comprehension of the work being performed. You can research many topics on Amazon or the web.

- The Concierge Manual
- The Concierge: Key to Hospitality
- The Lucky Shopping Manual
- The Modern Gentleman: A Guide to Essential Manners, Savvy & Vice
- The Insider's Guide to Household Staffing
- How to Be a Gentleman: A Contemporary Guide to Common Courtesy
- A Gentleman's Guide to Etiquette
- Behavior in Public Places
- Fabulous Gifts: Hollywood's Gift Guru Reveals Secret to Giving Perfect Present
- Butlers & Household Managers: 21st Century Professionals
- The Organizer : Secrets & Systems from the World's Top Executive Assistants
- The Valuable Office Professional
- Administrative Assistant's and Secretary's Handbook
- The New Office Professional's Handbook
- Strengths-Based Leadership
- The Art of Speed Reading People
- Do What You Are: Discover the Perfect Career for You
- Change Your Life in Seven Days
- Instant Confidence

- The Power of Charm

On The Job Training

Every day is a learning experience. You will no doubt learn many things while on the job. Did you know that a tire filled with nitrogen retains optimal pressure longer, leading to more uniform tire wear and better gas mileage? Or that peanut butter used in a mouse trap does not do as good a job as peanut shells? Or if a parking meter says "fail" you are allowed to park there for a minimum of thirty minutes? There are many things you will learn on the job. Some as silly as these and some more valuable that you can take with you anywhere. One of the most important things you will learn on the job is your limitations. Use your creativity to push passed it. You will grow with every challenge. Don't be afraid to step up to the plate and swing.

Insightful Magazines

Every industry has a magazine that is useful to that business. Depending on what your employer does, you can always find magazines which give you current information on that industry. If you employer doesn't subscribe, you may want to think about suggesting it to him or even subscribing to the online version.

There are even magazines that may be useful to you and your job:

RealSimple	Food & Wine
Sunset	Bon Appetite
Vogue	Gourmet
In Style	Time
Elle	Entertainment Weekly
GQ	Sports Illustrated
Travel & Leisure	ESPN
Architectural Digest	Women's Health
Better Homes &	Men's Fitness
Gardens	

Depending on your employer's field of endeavor and his personal interests, some magazines for him or her may include;

Inc. 5000	Wired
Fortune	Scientific American
Time	Variety
Money	Hollywood Reporter
HR	Vanity Fair
Entrepreneur	LA Confidential
Forbes	The New Yorker
Fast Company	The Atlantic
The Economist	Town & Country
The Nation	Smithsonian
Huffington Post	Condé Nast Traveller

Chapter 17:
The Invaluable Bible

Of the many tools of the trade you will use, a number of Personal Assistants have found the bible to be one of the most invaluable tools in your arsenal. Not only can it save you hours of pain and headache, but you will be able to make it available for anyone in the household to reference and it can also make your job really convenient.

What Is The Bible?

Simply put, the bible (Household Management Reference Book) is a collection of everything that is important to running and maintaining the household and/or the office. If created properly, it gives you answers to most situations right at your fingertips. You can know on the fly who to call if the power goes out, where the water main is kept should there be a major leak or pipe breakage. You can list everything from important travel information to passport numbers, expiration dates, birthdates, purchase dates of equipment and household items, warranty information, what to do in an emergency, emergency contact numbers for doctors, schools, auto, and more.

If you have the capability, the bible can keep a colored photo copy of credit cards (front and back), insurance records, passports, driver's license, frequent flyer cards, auto registration and much, much more.

The purpose of the bible is that when you need important information it can be obtained quickly and it also frees you up to do other important tasks. Instead of calling you late at night and asking where something is or how to light the pilot on the fireplace, the user can simply refer to the

"How To" section of the bible to see the step by step instructions.

At the bottom of every bible page, is an automated mechanism that puts the most *current date* when the page was last modified. This way you can keep on top of your updates and know how current the information is.

Some employers may freak out about having a bible at first. Assure them that it will be kept in a safe, protected place and will NEVER leave the premises. Show them what it can really do. Illustrate the benefits of having a household bible to them. In the beginning, you can start small, just having basic contacts, and *how to* items, like where the breaker box is located. How to turn the fireplace on and off. How to work the various remote controls. Keep a list of favorite restaurants you often book reservations for. How about auto information? Where do you service the cars? When was the last time the vehicles were taken for an oil change or tune-up? List home and auto insurance information and who your agent is. Upcoming birthdays. Frequent flyer numbers, fax numbers, names of doctors, etc.

In the beginning you could always start with having the bible only on your computer with a locked password requirement. But ultimately the purpose of having the bible available is to assist whoever is at the household and sometimes if you are away and traveling it may be necessary for the maid, butler, chef, Second Assistant, or nanny to know how to reset a blown fuse or who the plumber is and how to reach them.

Laminated List Of Important Contacts

Another valuable tool in your bag of tricks is laminated contact cards. Again, you will find a template included on the *Additional Tools to Download* page at the end of this guide.

Here you will have a list at hand of contractors, insurance, auto, TV services, pool maintenance, housekeeper, or any of the important numbers that you use on an hourly, daily, or weekly basis.

You can modify this contact card however you'd like, but you'll notice that restaurants are listed on the front of the card.

On the back side is additional important information such as doctors (which are best kept separate from the contractors on the front side), school info if there are children, their friends, the parents and all the important phone numbers and addresses. There is also Auto information, office info, and personal contacts. But again, you can modify this to cater to your household needs.

Where do you use these cards? Since they are quick reference, they're best kept beside every phone in the household, and sometimes also in each vehicle. You are probably saying, what if they get taken from the cars? The cards are usually kept out of sight and in many years of experience, not one card was ever taken or went missing from a vehicle.

Again, use Microsoft Word's auto date feature to notate at the bottom of the page the last update. This contact card should be updated every six to eight months.

Print it out on a white piece of paper, double-sided, by running it through your printer twice. Then you can laminate them at Kinko's using a 10 Mil laminate.

Up-To-Date Contact Database

One of the most important parts of your job will be to keep the most updated list of important personal and business contacts. It would be wise to take a week out of each year and contact every person and business contact on the list to make sure you have their most current information. You'll want to ask them for their address, phone, fax, email, assistants, mailing address (if different), cell number and home address.

Very often a cell phone will change; someone will purchase a new home or move to a new office location. A couple you know can divorce and have several new addresses and phone numbers.

Once you've obtained this information, you can then incorporate it into both the bible and the contact cards. While this isn't for everyone, some households will make good use of these. It's also great to use for holiday, special occasions, gifts, and cards.

Palm vs. Blackberry vs. Windows vs. Paper?

There is no substitute for paper. That being said, there will be times when your new boss will be all about using the Blackberry and you use a palm. There are workarounds for this but they can be a pain. At some point you may have to acquiesce and get the same type of device as your boss.

Since Blackberry will be staying in business after the court rulings, there are still as many people who prefer it as there are people who use the Palm or other PDA devices. Apple has the *iPhone*. Even Microsoft is also getting into the mix, and Palm is releasing their new *Pre*. There are lots of choices out there for handheld users.

The best thing for you is to get acquainted with all the devises at least in a very rudimental way so you won't lag behind when you start a new job.

It might be helpful if you are using a search or placement agency to find your jobs, to ask them what type of technical devices the people use who are hiring the Personal Assistant.

Part 5: Employer's Guide

Chapter 18:
Tips Every Employer Needs!

What Kind of Assistant Is Right For You?

How many Personal Assistants have you gone through? Perhaps this is your first Personal Assistant and you don't know what to look for or what to expect.

The kind of Personal Assistant you want will almost always be someone whose personality matches or is similar to your own. Keep in mind that you will be working with this person day in and out and sometimes you will be together more than you are with a spouse.

The second thing you need to look for is someone who can meet your needs. The best way to do this is to write up a task list of everything you think will be required of the Personal Assistant. Imagine your day. What areas of assistance would benefit you the most? Will there be driving involved? Do you hop a lot? Will the Personal Assistant be picking up alterations or gifts purchased? Running errands? Picking up children? Managing the household? The more specific you can be with what your needs are, the better match you will find in a Personal Assistant.

Even the amount of time you think it will take for them to do their job every day will help you to determine what type of Personal Assistant you'll need. Do you require someone to stay busy all the time or is it more important that someone is always at the house keeping an eye on everything? Maybe the type of Personal Assistant you need is someone who can travel with you and keep you company.

Beginning Your Search

You will get recommendations from friends, relatives and associates. Resist the urge to immediately hire from these pools if you can. You may want to hire one of these referrals because you think you can save some money or because the person being recommended is from a trusted source. In the long run you may end up just wasting both money and valuable time. Also, keep in mind that while the person being recommended may have been great for your friends, remember that a big part of successful hiring is choosing someone whose personality is suited to yours.

Another reason not to hire these types of people is that there can be resentment built by the Personal Assistant/Friend when a less favorable task needs to get done. Perhaps you hired a friend who you used to go to the movies with and invited to every occasion. You think it will be fun to hang out and travel together because you both have fun together. But then one day you're out having fun and your new Personal Assistant/Friend is upstairs in your closet collecting the clothes that need to go to the dry cleaner. And there will be times when you have personal things you would rather not have a friend know about. Another issue can be money. When they learn how much tedious work they have to do for you, they may begin to resent it, they can begin to think you are not paying them enough to go from social acquaintance to Personal Assistant. It's just better not to hire someone you know. Yes, there are always exceptions to the rule, but they *are* just that. Exceptions.

There are several agencies that can pre-screen your candidates and save you from hours of wasting interviewing time and headaches.

First Round of Interviews

Even though you have an agency prescreen, it is good to have someone on your team interview the candidate before they finally meet with you. This should be someone who knows and understands your habits, and tastes, and can objectively find someone who could work with you and "put up" with some of your quirks (even though you don't have any) on a daily basis.

Be careful when using an attorney to do the interviewing. Sometimes even though you've known your attorney for many years, he or she may not know or understand exactly what a good match for you means. While you may use them for the preliminary weeding out, you should have someone who really knows your tastes, likes and dislikes to do the second screening before the candidate ever meets with you.

When you do finally meet the candidate, notice how you feel around this person. Does she or he make you anxious? Or do they give you a sense of calm and protectiveness in your own environment? Read the section below on *Can I Trust My Instincts.*

How To Review A Resume

Longevity does say a lot. It tells you that the former employer trusted the Personal Assistant and felt comfortable with them handling the daily tasks and personal matters. However, sometimes longevity can also mean being stuck in a rut and not knowing the best exit strategy. This can go for both the employee and the employer.

Pay attention to the order the candidate lists their duties. This can often tell you their strong suits. The ones listed first are often times the ones they perform the best.

Pay attention to the wording. How they write their resume can also give insight into how well they will write for you. If this is an issue for you and you're someone who needs a capable writer, then you need to take notice.

Can I Trust My Instincts?

You should always trust your instincts. Two-thirds of why you hire someone is based on your instincts. The rest is based on recommendation or work history. Now you are going to say that you've hired some bad people in the past. Was that based on a recommendation of a friend? Was it their resume that caught your attention? Or did you listen to your instincts about the person? Trust yourself and rely on your gut. However, this doesn't mean that the candidate doesn't have to first earn your trust. You shouldn't just hand over the keys to fort Knox. You will still need to take it slowly and see how things progress. Also, you should always have a confidentiality agreement, signed before the first day of the new position. You're allowing someone access to your private and personal world and you need to protect it. Yes you are hiring someone who you will have to trust, but you wouldn't go to New York and leave your purse open would you? You need to be proactive and having a confidentiality agreement can save you from any worries or headaches down the road. Remember, it's just business, and once business is out of the way you can relax and enjoy your life knowing you have someone responsible looking after your affairs.

What Is Fair Compensation?

Chapter 4 contains a rough guideline to help people understand what is fair compensation for the duties and tasks that will be required of the Personal Assistant. Since a lot of people in the entertainment business have business managers, You might be clueless about what *fair* compensation is. Use this guide or ask the placement agency, but if you ask a friend or even your attorney, they too can be clueless in this matter.

Show your appreciation. It can go a long way. Communicate with your Personal Assistant. You may even want to have periodic sit-downs to make sure you're both on the same page.

Build trust carefully. You are giving them a lot of power when they first come on board. The best thing to do when bringing a new Personal Assistant into your home or business is to start with petty cash. Have them give you a weekly report listing everything they purchased or spent money on and have it include receipts that match the expenses. Some employers don't want to go through this hassle so you can also consider getting them a credit card with a spending cap. This can be a good way to build trust and keep an eye on your world. Do not assume everyone is good. Just because you hired them and brought them into your private world, you still need to take the time to build a rapport and trust base between the two of you. Even if it's someone who you've hired through a referral of a close friend or associate, you still need to establish a trust base.

Agencies to Help Your Search

Here is a list of reputable Placement Agencies and Professional Headhunters who can help you with your search for a Personal Assistant that's a right match for you. Most agencies will do an extensive review and screening process of the candidate before ever putting them before you. You should also ask if they provide a background check to further weed out the unwanted.

Kerri Campos Consulting:
www.kerricampos.com
International Services Agency:
www.isastaffing.com
Lifestyle Resources:
www.sterlinglifestyle.com
Starkey International Institute:
www.starkeyintl.com
The Grapevine Agency:
www.thegrapevinela.com
CPAI:
www.celebritypersonalassistants.com
Comar Agency:
www.comaragency.com
Christopher Baker Staffing :
www.christopherbakerstaffing.com
The Elizabeth Rose Agency:
www.elizabethroseagency.com
The Robin Kellner Agency:
www.robinkellner.com

Best Domestic Placement Services:
www.bestdomestic.com
Celebrities Staffing Services:
www.canyceleb-staffing.com
Colonial Domestic Agency:
www.colonialdomestics.com
Mahler Enterprises, Inc:
www.mahlerent.com
RWP Solutions:
www.rwpsolutions.com
The Calendar Group:
www.thecalendargroup.com
The Help Company:
www.thehelpcompany.com
The Katie Facey Agency:
www.katiefaceyagency.com
Elite Domestic Agency:
www.elitedomesticagency.com
Miranda of Beverly Hills Domestic Agency:
www.mirandaofbeverlyhills.com

Chapter 19:
A Final Thought For The Seasoned And Not-So-Seasoned

Take pride in your work. Use the tools provided in this guide. Excel and work hard. But most of all enjoy your life. Don't forget that you don't live to work, you work to live. Take a moment to appreciate the things around you. You may not know it but a big part of why you were hired in the first place is due to the life experiences you've gathered. Your outlook on life and the world, your manners, behaviors towards others, how you feel, think, and breathe.

Spend time with the people you care most about. Go to a concert. Travel. Seek out a restaurant you are passionate about and enjoy every bite of food, and every sip of wine. Walk through your favorite museum. Take a drive along the coast, or through the mountains. Sleep in. Take a picnic to the park, lay on the grass and look at the clouds. Take your shoes off and walk in the hot sand along the beach. Buy yourself a piece of chocolate and savor the moment. Share a glass of wine. Go to a bar and watch your favorite team. Head to Las Vegas. Read books and magazines. Go to the movies and don't forget the popcorn. Volunteer at some charity organization. Buy yourself a gift.

Once you have done any or all of the above, you are ready to work as a successful Personal Assistant because your present or future boss will see a light inside of you and know you are a force to be reckoned with. You are someone who is in control, who understands what it takes to have a successful, fulfilling life. You are someone they can't do without having on their team. You are the next, successful Personal Assistant. Congratulations.

About The Author

I've worked for A-list actors, Grammy winning performers, heads of major corporations, top producers, directors, and entrepreneurs. I landed one coveted Personal Assistant position by being the first of fifty people to find a rare exotic car (one of only three hundred made). I scored a private box for a Madonna concert one day before the concert, and when my employer wasn't happy with the location, I was able to get a second, more coveted, private box on the day of the concert. I've lived on a secluded island with moguls like Paul Allen. I've flown in everything from puddle jumpers to private jets, Citation Tens, Gulfstream IV & Vs, to the now retired Concord, the fastest commercial plane. I've also washed dishes for eighty, cooked for twelve, thrown parties together for 200-1000 people, arranged transportation for an Ocelot (an American wildcat), shopped at the top fashion stores in Los Angeles and New York, held off a screaming mob of fans, held someone's hand while they were getting a tattoo, and changed diapers, light bulbs on the front porch, and the oil in a car. The point is, I've done a number of jobs both large and small and learned to take pride in every task given to me. It's what is and will be expected of you as a Personal Assistant.

Resources

Tools Of The Trade

Career Info:

Do What You Are: Discover the Perfect Career for You
(Amazon)

Cleaning:

How to Clean Anything – Online Authority for Free
Cleaning Information
www.howtocleananything.com

Concierge Tips:

The Concierge Manual
(Amazon)

The Concierge: Key to Hospitality
(Amazon)

Databases:

IMDB – Internet Movie Database
us.imdb.com

Who Represents – Contact info for Celebrities and their
Representatives
www.whorepresents.com

Entertainment:

Seeing Stars.com – Celebrity Events and Happenings
www.seeing-stars.com/Calendar

Visualnet - The Film, TV & Video Production Link
www.visualnet.com

Etiquette:

Complete Guide to Executive Manners
(Amazon)

The Modern Gentleman: A Guide to Essential Manners,
Savvy & Vice
(Amazon)

How to Be a Gentleman: A Contemporary Guide to
Common Courtesy
(Amazon)

A Gentleman's Guide to Etiquette
(Amazon)

Everything Legal:

Forms Guru – Legal Forms
www.findlegalforms.com

How Things:

eHow – How Things get Done (tying a tie, negotiate a
raise, win at Monopoly)
www.ehow.com

How Stuff Works – Info on how almost everything
works
www.howstuffworks.com

Consumer Search – Info about Products and how they
perform
www.consumersearch.com

Managing A Household:

Butlers & Household Managers: 21st Century
Professionals
(Amazon)

The Insider's Guide to Household Staffing
(Amazon)

Organizing:

The Organizer : Secrets & Systems from the World's Top Executive Assistants
(Amazon)

Parties & Events:

Party Planning – Everything for putting on a Party
www.party411.com

References:

RefDesk – Fact Checker for the Internet
www.refdesk.com

Restaurant Reservations:

Open Table – Restaurant Reservation Booking
www.opentable.com

Self Improvement:

Change Your Life in Seven Days
(Amazon)

Instant Confidence
(Amazon)

The Power of Charm
(Amazon)

Behavior in Public Places
(Amazon)

Strengths-Based Leadership
(Amazon)

The Art of Speed Reading People
(Amazon)

Shopping:

Paris Personal Shopper
parispersonalshopper.susantabak.com/

The Lucky Shopping Manual
(Amazon)

Fabulous Gifts: Giving Perfect Present
(Amazon)

The Office:

The Valuable Office Professional
(Amazon)

Administrative Assistant's and Secretary's Handbook
(Amazon)

The New Office Professional's Handbook
(Amazon)

Travel:

Trip.com – Deals on Travel Rates and Prices
www.trip.com

Travel & Leisure – Hotels, Restaurants, Destinations
www.travelandleisure.com

Training Services:

Starkey International Institute
www.starkeyintl.com

Kerri Campos Consulting
www.kerricampos.com

PDSI
www.housestaff.net

CPAI
www.celebritypersonalassistants.com

Lifestyle Resources
www.sterlinglifestyle.com

Additional Tools to Download:

With the purchase of this guide you will have access to many downloadable templates to help make your job more efficient and run smoothly.

Please contact info@personalassistantguide.com and give your name, email, and sales confirmation code. You will be sent an email with the url and access code to download and unlock these templates.

> ➢ Household Bible (How to find/operate things, important numbers, contacts, travel, and auto info fast) (Access Code: 555555)
> ➢ Monthly Calendar
> ➢ Call Sheet
> ➢ Expense Report
> ➢ FedEx Log
> ➢ Gift List
> ➢ Grocery List
> ➢ Household Numbers
> ➢ Limousine Request Sheet
> ➢ Non-Disclosure Agreement
> ➢ Daily Projects
> ➢ Purchase Records
> ➢ Travel Checklist
> ➢ Travel Itinerary
> ➢ Weekly Project Schedule
> ➢ Weekly Restocking List
> ➢ Weekly To Do List
> ➢ Xmas List